FORTY CENTURIES
OF
WAGE AND PRICE
CONTROLS:
How Not To Fight Inflation

FORTY CENTURIES

OF

WAGE AND PRICE CONTROLS:

How <u>Not</u> To Fight Inflation

Robert L. Schuettinger
Eamonn F. Butler

With a Foreword by
David I. Meiselman

The Heritage Foundation

Washington, D.C.

Distributed by
Caroline House, Publishers, Inc.

Thornwood, New York

Short excerpts from *Forty Centuries of Wage and Price Controls: How Not to Fight Inflation* have been previously published in the following formats:

Robert L. Schuettinger, *A Brief Survey of Wage and Price Controls From 2800 B.C. to A.D. 1952* (Washington, D.C.: The Heritage Foundation, 1974).

Robert L. Schuettinger, "Have Controls Ever Worked? The Historical Record: A Survey of Wage and Price Controls Over Fifty Centuries" in *The Illusion of Wage and Price Control* (Michael Walker, editor) (Vancouver, Canada: The Fraser Institute, 626 Bute Street, Vancouver, British Columbia, V6E 3M1, Canada, 1976).

Robert L. Schuettinger, "Wage-Price Control, The First 5,000 Years," in *Wage-Price Control: Myth and Reality* (Sudha Shenoy, editor) (Turramurra, Australia: The Centre for Independent Studies, P.O. Box 32, Turramurra, 2074, Australia, 1978).

Robert L. Schuettinger, "Four Thousand Years of Wage and Price Controls," *Policy Review*, Summer 1978.

Eamonn Butler, "How Government Profits From Inflation," *Policy Review*, Fall 1978.

The co-authors wish to thank Mr. Jeff MacNelly (holder of two Pulitzer Prizes) of *The Richmond News-Leader* and his syndicate, the Chicago Tribune-New York News Syndicate, for permission to reprint ten of his cartoons. These cartoons are copyrighted (1978) by the Chicago Tribune-New York News Syndicate.

Library of Congress Cataloging in Publication Data

78-74609

ISBN 0-89195-023-0 (paper back)
ISBN 0-89195-025-7 (hard cover)

Published by The Heritage Foundation
513 C. St., N.E.
Washington, D.C. 20002

Distributed to the Book Trade
by Caroline House, Publishers, Inc.
P.O. Box 161
Thornwood, N.Y. 10594

For
Milton and Rose Friedman

ROBERT L. SCHUETTINGER is Director of Studies of The Heritage Foundation and editor of its quarterly journal, *Policy Review*. He was recently elected to the presidency of a national association of university professors (UPAO).

Educated in a one-room schoolhouse in Charlotte, Vermont, he later studied under Nobel Laureate F. A. Hayek at the Committee on Social Thought of the University of Chicago, under Sir Isaiah Berlin, O.M. at Oxford University and at Columbia University; he has taught at The Catholic University of America, St. Andrews University and Yale University, where he was also a visiting fellow of Davenport College.

Schuettinger also served four years as a Senior Research Associate with the Republican Study Committee in the U.S. Congress. He is the editor of *The Conservative Tradition in European Thought*, the author of *Lord Acton: Historian of Liberty, Saving Social Security* and *A Research Guide in Public Policy*. He is also the co-author of *U.S. National Security Policy in the Decade Ahead* and of four other books on foreign policy.

EAMONN F. BUTLER recently was awarded the Ph.D. degree from St. Andrews University in Scotland. He has served as a senior aide in economic policy in the U.S. House of Representatives and has taught economics at Hillsdale College, Michigan. He is the co-author (with his brother, Stuart) of *The British National Health Service*.

DAVID I. MEISELMAN, the author of the Foreword, is Professor of Economics and Director of the Northern Virginia Graduate Program at Virginia Polytechnic Institute and State University. He has served as a senior economist with the U.S. Congress and is the author of several books, including *Varieties of Monetary Experience*.

Table of Contents

Foreword

Attempts to control and fix prices and wages span most of recorded history. As Robert Schuettinger and Eamonn Butler record in such illuminating and interesting detail in this book, price and wage controls cover the times from Hammurabi and ancient Egypt 4,000 years ago to this morning's newspaper accounts of rent controls in New York, Boston and other U.S. cities, the Carter Administration's program of "voluntary" price controls, the mandatory price and wage controls in Norway, Denmark and Iran, and so forth.

The experience under price controls is as vast as essentially all of recorded history, which gives us an unparalleled opportunity to explore what price controls do and do not accomplish. I know of no other economic and public policy measure whose effects have been tested over such diverse historical experience in different times, places, peoples, modes of government and systems of economic organization—except perhaps for studies of the relationship between inflation and increases in the quantity of money.*

The results of this investigation would merit attention for the light it sheds on economic and political phenomena even if wage and price controls were no longer seriously considered as tools of economic policy. The fact that wage and price controls exist in many countries and markets and are being seriously considered by others, including the United States, compels attention to the historical record of wage and price controls this book presents.

What, then, have price controls achieved in the recurrent struggle to restrain inflation and overcome shortages? The historical record is a grimly uniform sequence of repeated failure. Indeed, there is not a single episode where price controls have worked to stop inflation or cure shortages. Instead of curbing inflation, price controls add other complications to the inflation disease, such as black markets and shortages that reflect the waste and misallocation of resources caused by the price controls themselves. Instead of eliminating shortages, price controls cause or worsen shortages. By giving producers and consumers the wrong signals because "low"

---

*For an excellent summary, see Anna J. Schwartz, "Secular Price Change in Historical Perspective," Universities-National Bureau Committee for Economic Research, Conference on Secular Inflation, supplement to *Journal of Money, Credit and Banking*, February 1973, p. 264.

prices to producers limit supply and "low" prices to consumers stimulate demand, price controls widen the gap between supply and demand.

Despite the clear lessons of history, many governments and public officials still hold the erroneous belief that price controls can and do control inflation. They thereby pursue monetary and fiscal policies that cause inflation, convinced that the inevitable cannot happen. When the inevitable does happen, public policy fails and hopes are dashed. Blunders mount, and faith in governments and government officials whose policies caused the mess declines. Political and economic freedoms are impaired and general civility suffers.

Many of the results of price controls, such as black and gray markets, are predictable and have the inevitability of mathematics and of many of the laws of the physical sciences. Nations that ignore them are no less periled than those that decree that two plus two must equal three, that the Pythagorean Theorem is false or promulgate laws that limit the temperature of steam to 40° (F or C).

First-hand experience of most of us with wage and price controls in our own lifetimes in addition to the lessons of history and of validated propositions in economics so skillfully catalogued in this book would seem to be more than sufficient to convince the public and government officials that price and wage controls simply do not work. However, the unpleasant reality is that, despite all the evidence and analyses, many of us still look to price controls to solve or to temper the problem of inflation. Repeated public opinion polls show that a majority of U.S. citizens would prefer to have mandatory controls. If the polls are correct, and I have no reason to doubt them, it must mean that many of us have not yet found out what forty centuries of history tell us about wage and price controls. Alternatively, it raises the unpleasant question, not why price controls do not work, but why, in spite of repeated failures, governments, with the apparent support of many of their citizens, keep trying.

This book makes a most valuable and timely contribution to our knowledge and to the ongoing discussion of important public policy issues. It is profoundly to be hoped that we can learn enough from forty centuries of wage and price controls to avoid dooming ourselves to repeating their certain and costly failures.

DAVID I. MEISELMAN
Virginia Polytechnic Institute
and State University

Preface

The co-authors began working on this book in 1974, just after the termination of President Nixon's controls in the United States. Since that time, we have examined over one hundred cases of wage and price controls in thirty different nations from 2000 B.C. to A.D. 1978.

Naturally, we were only able to provide in one book a brief survey of so broad a subject. To our knowledge, however, this is the only history of wage and price controls in the major nations of the world in one volume. We hope, therefore, that the data we have gathered and analyzed and the ten page bibliography we have compiled will be of use to scholars wishing to do further work on more specialized aspects of the history of inflation and of government economic controls.

We have concluded that, while there have been some cases in which controls have at least apparently curtailed the effects of inflation for a short time, they have always failed in the long run. The basic reason for this is that they have not addressed the real cause of inflation which is an increase in the money supply over and above the increase in productivity. Rulers from the earliest times sought to solve their financial problems by debasing the coinage or issuing almost worthless coins at high face values; through modern technology the governments of recent centuries have had printing presses at their disposal. When these measures resulted in inflation, the same rulers then turned to wage and price controls.

After forty (or more) centuries, the problem is still with us. Recent polls reveal that the overwhelming majority of the American people regard inflation as the most important problem facing the country today.* Professor Karl Brunner of the University of Rochester and many other prominent economists now believe that we may be in an era of permanent inflation, that is, that the United States and Western Europe may be burdened by the kind of high and persistent inflation rates previously confined to Latin American nations. As a result of the current double-digit inflation, the latest Harris Poll (October 1978) indicates that 58 percent of the people now favor mandatory wage and price controls.

---

*The same view is held in Britain and a number of other industrialized nations. Inflation is obviously a worldwide problem, so it is not inappropriate that one of the authors (Schuettinger) is an American and the other (Butler) is British.

Naturally, we hope that those who read this book will come to conclude that controls are not the solution to the problem of inflation.

There can be little doubt that if a workable solution is not implemented in the near future the lives of most of us (and perhaps more importantly, the lives of our children) will be changed for the worse. The distinguished political commentator, David S. Broder, writing in *The Boston Globe* (October 25, 1978) put into eloquent and compelling language the dangers now facing us.

> What inflation has done fundamentally [he wrote] is to deepen the insecurities in this country, and thus warp the opportunities for positive leadership on other issues . . . inflation damages the conservative social values which are essential to the country's future. Stability, savings and investment are all undermined by inflation. Severe inflation makes a mockery of most families' financial plans. Most working people feel there is no way they can protect their budgets against this kind of assault on the dollar.
>
> It erodes the sense of trust on which an economy and a society rest, and it makes people cynical about the chances of attaining any social goal more ambitious than mere survival.
>
> While it persists, there will hardly be room in our politics for any other major issue.

If, by writing this book, we are able to make a small contribution to the debate on this crucial issue and to move our countries a few steps forward to a realistic solution to this all-pervasive problem, our efforts will have been repaid.

Both the co-authors consulted each other on the chapters written by each and take responsibility for the book as a whole. Andrew Chalk, recently a Walker Fellow in economics at The Heritage Foundation and now a Ph.D. candidate at Washington University in St. Louis, did much of the research and wrote a first draft for Chapters 9 and 10 (on Germany and the Soviet Union). Eamonn F. Butler wrote the chapters on economic analysis (Chapters 12, 14, 16, 17, 18 and 19) while the co-authors jointly wrote Chapters 13 and 15. Robert L. Schuettinger primarily wrote the remaining, mainly historical, chapters.

The co-authors wish to thank several persons who made contributions, in various ways, to the final work. We are especially grateful to Edwin J. Feulner, Jr., the President of The Heritage Foundation, who initially suggested the idea of such a book to Schuettinger five years ago when they were both on the staff of the U.S. Congress; since that time he has retained a strong interest in the expansion and completion of what began as a short essay and he has taken an active role in seeing the book gradually assume finished form through several stages. Other persons who helped to make this a better book than it would otherwise be include: Herb Berkowitz,

Jameson Campaigne, Jr., Beverly Childers, Marion Green, Eugene McAllister, Charles Moser, Hugh C. Newton, Richard Odermatt, Shirley Starbuck, John J. Tierney, Jr., Phil N. Truluck, and Richard S. Wheeler.

Naturally, there is no honorable way for the co-authors to shift responsibility for any remaining shortcomings to anyone but themselves.

ROBERT L. SCHUETTINGER
Burlington, Vermont

EAMONN F. BUTLER
St. Andrews, Scotland

February 12, 1979

7

Inflation Results When Money Increases Faster Than Output

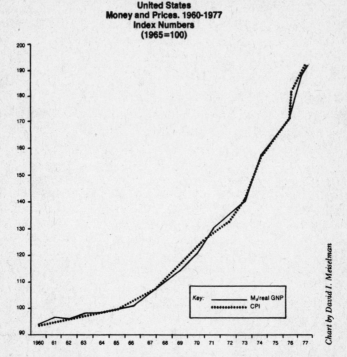

United States
Money and Prices. 1960-1977
Index Numbers
(1965=100)

Key: ———— M₂/real GNP
•••••••••••• CPI

Chart by David I. Meiselman

(Sources: CPI, *Monthly Labor Review;* GNP, *Economic Report of The President;* Money Supply (M₂), *Federal Reserve Bulletin*).

The above chart illustrates the close connection, since 1960, between the U.S. Consumer Price Index and the ratio of money to output using the broad M₂ measure of money (M₂ equals currency in the hands of the public and all bank deposits less large certificates of deposit). The close connection noted above has been traced back by economists through at least the last 400 years of recorded economic history.

For a full explanation of this and related phenomena see David I. Meiselman's chapter "Worldwide Inflation: A Monetarist View," in *The Phenomenon of Worldwide Inflation,* edited by David I. Meiselman and Arthur B. Laffer, (Washington, D.C.: The American Enterprise Institute, 1975).

See also Chapter Three ("Monetary Correction") in Milton Friedman's latest book, *Tax Limitation, Inflation and the Role of Government* (Dallas: The Fisher Institute, 12810 Hillcrest Road, Dallas, Texas, 75230, 1978). This chapter was originally published in *Fortune,* July 1974.

1

The Ancient World

From the earliest times, from the very inception of organized government, rulers and their officials have attempted, with varying degrees of success, to "control" their economies. The notion that there is a "just" or "fair" price for a certain commodity, a price which can and ought to be enforced by government, is apparently coterminous with civilization.

For the past forty-six centuries (at least) governments all over the world have tried to fix wages and prices from time to time. When their efforts failed, as they usually did, governments then put the blame on the wickedness and dishonesty of their subjects, rather than upon the ineffectiveness of the official policy. The same tendencies remain today.

The passion for economic planning, as Professor John Jewkes has cogently pointed out,[1] is perennial. Centralized planning regularly appears in every generation and is just as readily discarded after several years of fruitless experimentation, only to rise again on a subsequent occasion. Grandiose plans for regulating investment, wages, prices and production are usually unveiled with great fanfare and high hopes. As reality forces its way in, however, the plans are modified in the initial stages, then modified a little more, then drastically altered, then finally allowed to vanish quietly and unmourned. Human nature being what it is, every other decade or so the same old plans are dusted off, perhaps given a new name, and the process is begun anew.

IN THE LAND OF THE NILE

In the ancient world, of course, authority over the most important economic commodity, foodstuffs, was power indeed. "The man, or class of men, who controls the supply of essential foods is in possession of the supreme power. The safeguarding of the food supply has therefore been the concern of governments since they have been in existence," wrote Mary Lacy in 1922.[2] And as far back as the fifth dynasty in Egypt, generally dated about 2830 B.C. or earlier, the Monarch Henku had inscribed on his tomb, "I was lord and overseer of southern grain in this nome."

For centuries the Egyptian government strived to maintain control of the grain crop, knowing that control of food is control of lives. Using the pretext of preventing famine, the government gradually regulated more and more of the granaries; regulation led to direction and finally to outright ownership; land became the property of the monarch and was rented from him by the agricultural class.[3]

Under the Lagid dynasty (founded by Ptolemy I Soter in 306 B.C.) "there was a real omnipresence of the state. . . .The state . . . intervened by employing widely all its public law prerogatives . . . all prices were fixed by fiat at all levels."[4] According to the French historian, Jean-Philippe Lévy, "Control took on frightening proportions. There was a whole army of inspectors. There was nothing but inventories, censuses of men and animals . . . estimations of harvests to come. . . . In villages, when farmers who were disgusted with all these vexations ran away, those who remained were responsible for absentees' production . . . [one of the first effects of harsh price controls on farm goods is the abandonment of farms and the consequent fall in the supplies of food]. The pressure [the inspectors] applied extended, in case of need, to cruelty and torture."[5]

Egyptian workers during this period suffered badly from the abuses of the state intervention of the economy,[6] especially from the "bronze law," an economic theory which maintained that wages could never go above the bare necessities for keeping workers alive. The controls on wages set by the government reflected the prevailing economic doctrine.

"After a period of brilliance," Lévy concludes, "Egyptian economy collapsed at the end of the third century B.C., as did her political stability. The financial crisis was a permanency. Money was devalued. Alexandria's commerce declined. Workers, disgusted by the conditions imposed on them, left their lands and disappeared into the country. . . ."[7]

SUMERIA

In his very instructive work, *Must History Repeat Itself?*, Antony Fisher* calls our attention to a king of Sumeria,** Urakagina of Lagash, whose reign began about 2350 B.C. Urakagina, from the scanty records that have come down to us, was apparently a precursor of Ludwig Erhard, who began his rule by ending the burdens of excessive government regulations over the economy, including controls on wages and prices.

---

* For more very useful information on the sorry history of government interventions of all sorts in the economy (not only of wage and price controls) consult Antony Fisher's *Must History Repeat Itself?* (London: Churchill Press, 1974). (Published in the United States in 1978 by Caroline House, Ottawa, Ill.)

** Congressman Edward J. Derwinski of Illinois, who opposed the "Economic Stabilization Act" of 1971, inserted an interesting column by Jenkin Lloyd Jones (*Washington Star-News*, November 10, 1973) in the *Congressional Record* for November 12, 1973 (E7245). Mr. Jones pointed out some historical failures of controls, noting that "Efforts to fix prices for everything go back 41 centuries to the kings of ancient Sumer."

An historian of this period tells us that from Urakagina "we have one of the most precious and revealing documents in the history of man and his perennial and unrelenting struggle for freedom from tyranny and oppression. This document records a sweeping reform of a whole series of prevalent abuses, most of which could be traced to a ubiquitous and obnoxious bureaucracy . . . it is in this document that we find the word 'freedom' used for the first time in man's recorded history; the word is *amargi*, which . . . means literally 'return to the mother' . . . we still do not know why this figure of speech came to be used for 'freedom.' "[8]

BABYLON

In Babylon, some forty centuries ago, the Code of Hammurabi, the first of the great written law codes, imposed a rigid system of controls over wages and prices. Remembering the somewhat limited nature of the ancient economies (particularly those as ancient as the Babylonian), it is interesting to note the extent of wage controls imposed by the Hammurabi Code and the explicit way in which they are recorded. A few of the Articles of the Code (the complete statutes on wages and prices will be found in Appendix A) will suffice to illustrate this:*

> 257. If a man hire a field-labourer, he shall give him eight gur of corn per annum.
>
> 258. If a man hire a herdsman, he shall give him six gur of corn per annum.
>
> 261. If a man hire a pasturer for cattle and sheep, he shall give him eight gur of corn per annum.
>
> 268. If a man has hired an ox for threshing, twenty qa of corn is its hire.
>
> 269. If an ass has been hired for threshing, ten qa of corn is its hire.
>
> 270. If a young animal has been hired for threshing, one qa of corn is its hire.
>
> 271. If a man hire cattle, wagon, and driver, he shall give 180 qa of corn per diem.
>
> 272. If a man has hired a wagon by itself, he shall give forty qa of corn per diem.
>
> 273. If a man hire a workman, then from the beginning of the year until the fifth month he shall give six grains of silver per diem. From the sixth month until the end of the year he shall give five grains of silver per diem.

* Partially legible provisions have been omitted.

274. If a man hire a son of the people,
    Pay of a potter   five grains of silver,
    Pay of a tailor   five grains of silver,
    Pay of a carpenter   four grains of silver,
    Pay of a ropemaker   four grains of silver,
    he shall give per diem.

275. If a man hire a [illegible], her hire is three grains of silver per diem.

276. If a man hire a makhirtu, he shall give two and a half grains of silver per diem for her hire.

277. If a man hire a sixty-ton boat, he shall give a sixth part of a shekel of silver per diem for her hire.[9]

It is arguable that these controls blanketed Babylonian production and distribution, and smothered economic progress in the Empire, possibly for many centuries.[10]

Certainly the historical records show a decline in trade in the reign of Hammurabi and his successors. This was partly due to wage and price controls and partly due to the influence of a strong central government which intervened in most economic affairs in general. W. F. Leemans describes the recession as follows:

> Prominent and wealthy *tamkaru* (merchants) were no longer found in Hammurabi's reign. Moreover, only a few *tamkaru* are known from Hammurabi's time and afterwards . . . all . . . evidently minor tradesmen and money-lenders.[11]

In other words, it appears that the very people who were supposed to benefit from the Hammurabi wage and price restrictions were driven out of the market by those and other statutes.

The trade restrictions laid down by "Hammurabi, the protecting king . . . the monarch who towers above the kings of the cities . . ." as he called himself, were, to some extent, built upon the foundations of the social system developed under his predecessor, Rim-Sin. There was a remarkable change in the fortunes of the people of Nippur and Isin and the other ancient towns which he ruled, which came in the middle of Rim-Sin's reign. The beginning of the economic decline corresponds exactly with a series of "reforms" inaugurated by him. It appears that the noble monarch, after a series of impressive military victories, succeeded in having himself worshipped as a god, and henceforth took more political and economic power for his own administration and broke the influence of wealthy and influential traders. From thence, the number of *tamkaru* and wealthy men mentioned in the extant documents declines markedly. The number of property transactions for which records exist also diminishes. The number of administrative documents, which today we would call bureaucratic paperwork, simultaneously increases at a precipitous rate.[12]

THE OTHER SIDE OF THE WORLD

On the other side of the world, the rulers of ancient China shared the same paternalistic philosophy which was found among the Egyptians and Babylonians and would later be shared by the Greeks and Romans. In his study, *The Economic Principles of Confucius and His School*, the Chinese scholar, Dr. Huan-chang Chen, states that the economic doctrines of Confucius held that "government interference is necessary for economic life and competition should be reduced to a minimum."[13]

The Official System of Chou, for instance, was a handbook of government regulations for the use of mandarins of the Chou dynasty under which Confucius (born 552 B.C.) lived. According to Dr. Chen, there was detailed regulation of commercial life and prices were "controlled by the government." There was a large bureaucracy entrusted with this task; Dr. Chen relates that there was a master of merchants for every twenty shops and his duty was to establish the price of each item sold according to the cost. "When there is any natural calamity," he writes, "the merchants are not allowed to raise their price; for example, during a famine grain should be sold at the natural price [that is, at the price believed to be "natural" by the government] and during a great epidemic coffins should be sold in the same way."[14]

The officials of the ancient Chinese empire expected to do what members of their class have perennially attempted before and since: replace the natural laws of supply and demand with their own judgment, allegedly superior, of what the proper supply and demand *ought to be*. According to the official system of Chou (about 1122 B.C.), a superintendent of grain was appointed whose job was to survey the fields and determine the amount of grain to be collected or issued, in accordance with the condition of the crop, fulfilling the deficit of the demand and adjusting the supply. Indeed, lengthy economic "textbooks" on the subject of sensible grain management still exist from that time.

Dr. Chen comments laconically on this system in a footnote. "In modern times this policy has been changed to the opposite. During a famine, the price of grain is raised to induce merchants to bring in more grain."[15]

The regulations cited above, according to Dr. Chen, "were the actual rules under the Chou dynasty. In fact, in the classical time, the government did interfere with the commercial life very minutely."[16]

However, the results were not very favorable. "According to history," Dr. Chen notes, "whenever the government adopted any minute measure, it failed, with few exceptions. . . . since the Ch'in dynasty (221–206 B.C.), the government of modern China has not controlled the economic life of the people as did the government of ancient China."[17] Apparently, the Chinese mandarins did learn from experience.

Even in the classical period of Chinese history, however, there were a number of perceptive economists who saw the futility of government regulation of prices as a means of controlling inflation. In fact, they placed the blame for high prices squarely on the shoulders of the government itself. The economist Yeh Shih (A.D. 1150–1223), for instance, anticipated by several centuries the principle known as Gresham's Law in the West.

"The men who do not inquire into the fundamental cause," he wrote, "simply think that paper should be used when money is scarce. But as soon as paper is employed, money becomes still less. Therefore, it is not only that the sufficiency of goods cannot be seen, but also that the sufficiency of money cannot be seen."[18]

Another economist of about the same time, Yuan Hsieh (A.D. 1223), saw the principle even more clearly. He wrote:

> Now, the officials are anxious to increase wealth, and want to put both iron money and copper money in circulation. If money were suddenly made abundant during a period of scarcity, it should be very good. But the fact never can be so. Formerly, because the paper money was too much, the copper money became less. If we now add the iron money to it, should not the copper money but become still less? Formerly, because the paper money was too much, the price of commodities was dear. If we now add the iron money to the market, would the price not become still dearer? . . . When we look over the different provinces, the general facts are these. Where paper and money are both employed, paper is super-abundant, but money is always insufficient. Where the copper money is the only currency without any other money, money is usually abundant. Therefore, we know that the paper can only injure the copper money, but not help its insufficiency.[19]

Looking back at what we know to be the ineffectual history of government attempts to control inflation by regulating prices and wages, it is clear that these two Chinese economists of eight centuries ago were fully aware then of a law of economics that many political leaders have not learned to this day.

ANCIENT INDIA

A renowned Indian political philosopher known as Kautilya and sometimes as Vishnugupta was an influential king-maker who put the great Maurya Chandragupta on the throne in 321 B.C. He wrote the *Arthasastra*, the most famous of the ancient Indian "handbooks for Princes" as a guide to Chandragupta and other rulers; this collection of essays on the art of statesmanship contains much wise and perceptive advice.[20] However, like most government officials of his time and since, Kautilya could not forbear the practice of trying to regulate the economy on the lines he thought best.

In a chapter entitled "Protection Against Merchants," Kautilya outlined in some detail how the grain trade should be regulated and the levels of prices that merchants should be allowed to charge. He wrote:

14

. . . authorised persons alone. . . shall collect grains and other merchandise. Collections of such things without permission shall be confiscated by the superintendent of commerce.

Hence shall merchants be favourably disposed towards the people in selling grains and other commodities.

The superintendent of commerce shall fix a profit of five per cent over and above the fixed price of local commodities, and ten per cent on foreign produce. Merchants who enhance the price or realise profit even to the extent of half a pana more than the above in the sale or purchase of commodities shall be punished with a fine of from five panas in case of realising 100 panas up to 200 panas.

Fines for greater enhancement shall be proportionally increased. [21]

In a chapter entitled "Protection Against Artisans," Kautilya explains the "just" wages for a number of occupations, ranging from musicians to scavengers and concludes by saying, "Wages for the works of other kinds of artisans shall be similarly determined."[22]

Kautilya also recommends the appointment of government superintendents for a wide variety of economic activities, such as slaughterhouses, liquor supplies, agriculture and even ladies of the evening. For instance, there is a provision which states that "The superintendent shall determine the earnings . . . expenditure, and future earnings of every prostitute." There is a footnote for guidance which states very clearly that "Beauty and accomplishments must be the sole consideration in the selection of a prostitute."[23]

It is not known exactly how these price and wage regulations worked out in practice, but it would not be unreasonable to suppose that the end results were similar to what happened in Egypt, Babylon, Sumeria, China, Greece and other civilizations.

ANCIENT GREECE

Moving across another continent, we find that the Greeks behaved in just the same way. Xenophon[24] tells us that in Athens, a knowledge of the grain business was considered one of the qualities of a statesman. As a populous city-state with a small hinterland, Athens was constantly short of grain, at least half of which had to be imported from overseas. There was, needless to say, a natural tendency for the price of grain to rise when it was in short supply and to fall when there was an abundance. An army of grain inspectors, who were called *Sitophylakes*, was appointed for the purpose of setting the price of grain at a level the Athenian government thought to be just. It was a Golden Age consumer protection agency (of unusually large size for the period) whose duties were defined by Aristotle as

15

"to see to it first that the grain was sold in the market at a just price, that the millers sold meal in proportion to the price of barley, that the bakers sold bread in proportion to the price of wheat, that the bread had the weight they had fixed."[25]

The Professor of Ancient History at the University of Cambridge, M. I. Finley, comments in his recent study, *The Ancient Economy*, that

> Just price was a medieval concept, not an ancient one, and this interference by the state, altogether exceptional in its permanence, is a sufficient measure of the urgency of the food problem. And when this and all the other legislative measures I have mentioned on other occasions failed, the state, as a last recourse, appointed officials called *sitonai*, corn-buyers, who sought supplies wherever they could find them, raised public subscriptions for the necessary funds, introduced price reductions and rationing.[26]

The result was as might be expected: failure. Despite the penalty of death, which the harassed government did not hesitate to inflict, the laws controlling the grain trade were almost impossible to enforce. We have a surviving oration from at least one of the frustrated Athenian politicians who implored a jury to put the offending merchants to death.

He urged:

> But it is necessary, gentlemen of the Jury, to chastise them not only for the sake of the past, but also as an example for the future; for as things now are, they will hardly be endurable in the future. And consider that in consequence of this vocation, very many have already stood trial for their lives; and so great are the emoluments which they are able to derive from it that they prefer to risk their life every day, rather than cease to draw from you, the public, their improper profits. . . . If then, you shall condemn them, you shall act justly and you will buy grain cheaper; otherwise, the price will be much more.[27]

But Lysias was not the first and he was hardly the last politician to court popularity by promising the people lower prices in times of scarcity if only they would put an occasional merchant to the sword. The Athenian government, in fact, went so far as to execute its own inspectors when their price-enforcing zeal flagged. Despite the high mortality rates for merchants and bureaucrats alike, the price of grain continued to rise when supplies were short and continued to fall when supply was plentiful.

Regulatory agencies have had the same problems from time immemorial. T. F. Carney, in his informative book *The Economics of Antiquity*, has described the rise and the economic effect of ancient regulatory agencies in the following terms:

If a government and its key bureaucratic institutions can create a favourable environment for business, by the same token they can also do the reverse. Historically, economic development has been associated with public instrumentalities . . . .

. . . Bureaucrats [in the ancient world] were officials, with a punishment orientation towards their subject populations. . . . The government bureaucracy was regulative and extractive, not developmental. Originating in a scribal culture, it always tended to favour a mandarinate of literary generalists. There were no forces to countervail against it. Neither corporations, legislatures, nor political parties were yet in existence. In most cases, most of any society's tiny elite went into the apparatus of government. This government served an autocrat whose word was law. So there could be no constitutional safeguards for businessmen or against that apparatus . . . .[28]

And there is another way in which such ancient regulatory efforts show great parallels with contemporary ones. The *sitonai* were originally intended to be temporary, but as shortages arose from time to time (in no way abated by their work) there was a growing desire to keep them as permanent officials. If all else failed, Athenian colonial policy made it convenient enough to get rid of surplus citizens whom the regulated economy could not sustain. Some cynics might ask why some present-day economists have not thought of this solution to the commodity scarcities which inevitably follow upon price controls.[29]

FOOTNOTES

1. John Jewkes, *The New Ordeal By Planning* (London: MacMillan, 1948) *passim*.

2. Mary G. Lacy, *Food Control During Forty-Six Centuries* (Address before the Agricultural History Society, Washington, D.C., March 16, 1922) reprinted (Irvington-on-Hudson, New York: Foundation for Economic Education, Inc.) p. 2.

3. *Ibid.*, pp. 3–4.

4. Jean-Philippe Levy, *The Economic Life of the Ancient World* (Chicago: University of Chicago, 1967) pp. 40–41.

5. *Ibid.*, pp. 41–42.

6. *Ibid.*, pp. 42–43.

7. *Ibid.*, p. 43. For more information on the ancient Egyptian economy, see also M. I. Finley, *The Ancient Economy* (London: Chatto & Windus, 1973).

8. S. N. Kramer, *The Sumerians* (Chicago: University of Chicago, 1963) p. 79.

9. Chilperic Edwards, *The Hammurabi Code and the Sinaitic Legislation* (Port Washington, N.Y.: Kennikat Press, 1904) pp. 69–72. For the complete statutes on wages and prices from the *Code*, see Appendix A.

10. Irving S. Olds, *The Price of Price Controls* (Irvington-on-Hudson, New York: Foundation for Economic Education, 1952) p. 4.

11. W. F. Leemans, *The Old Babylonian Merchant*, Studia et Documenta (Leiden: E. F. Brill, 1950) p. 122.

12. *Ibid.*, pp. 114–115. See also James Wellard, *Babylon* (New York: Saturday Review Press, 1972).

13. Huan-chang Chen, *The Economic Principles of Confucius and His School* (New York: Longmans, 1911) p. 168.

14. *Ibid.*, p. 448.

15. *Ibid.*

16. *Ibid.*, p. 449.

17. *Ibid.*, p. 174.

18. *Ibid.*, p. 444.

19. *Ibid.*, pp. 444–445.

20. *Kautilya's Arthasastra* (Mysore: Wesleyan Mission Press, 1923) p. *v*.

21. *Ibid.*, p. 252.

22. *Ibid.*, p. 249.

23. *Ibid.*, p. 148.

24. August Boeckh, *The Public Economy of the Athenians*, translated by Anthony Lamb (Boston: Little Brown & Co., 1857) Book 1, Chapter 15.

25. Aristotle, *The Constitution of Athens*, 51.3.

26. Finley, *op. cit.*, p. 170.

27. Lysias, "Against the Grain Dealers" in Morris Morgan (ed.), *Eight Orations of Lysias* (Boston: Ginn & Co., 1895) pp. 89–103.

28. T. F. Carney, *The Economies of Antiquity* (Lawrence, Kansas: Coronado Press, 1973) pp. 35–36.

29. On regulation in the Hellenic economy, see Finley, *op. cit.*, Chapter VI.

2

The Roman Republic and Empire

As might be expected, the Roman Republic was not to be spared a good many ventures into control of the economy by the government. One of the most famous of the Republican statutes was the Law of the Twelve Tables (449 B.C.) which, among other things, fixed the maximum rate of interest at one uncia per libra (approximately 8 percent), but it is not known whether this was for a month or for a year. At various times after this basic law was passed, however, politicians found it popular to generously forgive debtors their agreed-upon interest payments. A Licinian law of 367 B.C., for instance, declared that interest already paid could be deducted from the principal owed, in effect setting a maximum price of zero on interest. The lex Genucia (342 B.C.) had a similar provision and we are told that violations of this "maximum" were "severely repressed under the lex Marcia." Levy concludes that "Aside from the Law of the Twelve Tables, these ad hoc or demagogic measures soon went out of use."[1]

The laws on grain were to have a more enduring effect on the history of Rome. From at least the time of the fourth century B.C., the Roman government bought supplies of corn or wheat in times of shortage and re-sold them to the people at a low fixed price. Under the tribune Caius Gracchus the Lex Sempronia Frumentaria was adopted which allowed every Roman citizen the right to buy a certain amount of wheat at an official price much lower than the market price. In 58 B.C. this law was "improved" to allow every citizen free wheat. The result, of course, came as a surprise to the government. Most of the farmers remaining in the countryside simply left to live in Rome without working.

Slaves were freed by their masters so that they, as Roman citizens, could be supported by the state. In 45 B.C. Julius Caesar discovered that almost one citizen in three was receiving his wheat at government expense. He managed to reduce this number by about half, but it soon rose again; throughout the centuries of the empire Rome was to be perpetually plagued with this problem of artifically low prices for grain, which caused economic dislocations of all sorts.[2]

In order to attempt to deal with their increasing economic problems, the emperors gradually began to devalue the currency. Nero (A.D. 54–68) began with small devaluations and matters became worse under Marcus Aurelius (A.D. 161–80) when the weights of coins were reduced. "These manipulations were the probable cause of a rise in prices," according to Levy. The Emperor

Commodus (A.D. 180–92) turned once again to price controls and decreed a series of maximum prices, but matters only became worse and the rise in prices became "headlong" under the Emperor Caracalla (A.D. 211–17).[3]

Egypt was the province of the Empire most affected, but her experience was reflected in lesser degrees throughout the Roman world. During the fourth century, the value of the gold solidus changed from 4,000 to 180 million Egyptian drachmai. Levy again attributes the phenomenal rise in prices which followed to the large increase of the amount of money in circulation. The price of the same measure of wheat rose in Egypt from 6 drachmai in the first century to 200 in the third century; in A.D. 314, the price rose to 9,000 drachmai and to 78,000 in A.D. 334; shortly after the year A.D. 344 the price shot up to more than 2 million drachmai. As noted, other provinces went through a similar, if not quite as spectacular, inflation.[4] Levy writes:

> In monetary affairs, ineffectual regulations were decreed to combat Gresham's Law [bad money drives out good] and domestic speculation in the different kinds of money. It was forbidden to buy or sell coins: they had to be used for payment only. It was even forbidden to hoard them! It was forbidden to melt them down (to extract the small amount of silver alloyed with the bronze). The punishment for all these offenses was death. Controls were set up along roads and at ports, where the police searched traders and travelers. Of course, all these efforts were to no purpose.[5]

THE EDICT OF DIOCLETIAN

The most famous and the most extensive attempt to control prices and wages occurred in the reign of the Emperor Diocletian who, to the considerable regret of his subjects, was not the most attentive student of Greek economic history. Since both the causes of the inflation that Diocletian attempted to control and the effects of his efforts are fairly well documented it is an episode worth considering in some detail.

Shortly after his assumption of the throne in A.D. 284, "prices of commodities of all sorts and the wages of laborers reached unprecedented heights." Historical records for determining the causes of this remarkable inflation are limited. One of the few surviving contemporary sources, the seventh chapter of the *De Moribus Persecutorum*, lays almost all the blame squarely at the feet of Diocletian. Since, however, the author is known to have been a Christian and since Diocletian, among other things, persecuted the Christians, we have to take this report *cum grano salis*. In this attack on the Emperor we are told that most of the economic troubles of the Empire were due to Diocletian's vast increase in the armed forces (there were several invasions by barbarian tribes during this period), to his huge building program (he rebuilt much of his chosen capital in Asia Minor, Nicomedia), to his consequent raising of taxes and the employment of more and more government officials and, finally, to his use of forced labor to accomplish much of his public works program.[6]

Diocletian himself, in his Edict (as we shall see) attributed the inflation entirely to the "avarice" of merchants and speculators.

A classical historian, Roland Kent, writing in the *University of Pennsylvania Law Review*, concludes from the available evidence that there were several major causes of the sharp rise in prices and wages. In the half century before Diocletian there had been a succession of short-reigned, incompetent rulers elevated by the military; this era of weak government resulted in civil wars, riots, general uncertainty and, of course, economic instability. There certainly was a steep rise in taxes, some of it justifiable for the defense of the Empire but some of it spent on grandiose public works of questionable value. As taxes rose, however, the tax base shrank and it became increasingly difficult to collect taxes, resulting in a vicious circle.[7]

It would seem clear that the major single cause of the inflation was the drastic increase in the money supply owing to the devaluation or debasement of the coinage. In the late Republic and early Empire, the standard Roman coin was the silver denarius; the value of that coin had gradually been reduced until, in the years before Diocletian, emperors were issuing tin-plated copper coins which were still called by the name "denarius." Gresham's Law, of course, became operative; silver and gold coins were naturally hoarded and were no longer found in circulation.

During the fifty-year interval ending with the rule of Claudius Victorinus in A.D. 268, the silver content of the Roman coin fell to one five-thousandth of its original level. With the monetary system in total disarray, the trade which had been a hallmark of the Empire was reduced to barter and economic activity was stymied. "The middle class was almost obliterated and the proletariat was quickly sinking to the level of serfdom. Intellectually the world had fallen into an apathy from which nothing would rouse it."[8] To this intellectual and moral morass came the Emperor Diocletian and he set about the task of reorganization with great vigor. Unfortunately, his zeal exceeded his understanding of the economic forces at work in the Empire.

In an attempt to overcome the paralysis associated with centralized bureaucracy, he decentralized the administration of the Empire and created three new centers of power under three "associate emperors." Since money was completely worthless, he devised a system of taxes based on payments in kind. This system had the effect, via the *ascripti glebae*, of totally destroying the freedom of the lower classes — they became serfs and were bound to the soil to ensure that the taxes would be forthcoming.

The "reforms" that are of most interest, however, are those relating to the currency and prices and wages. The currency reform came first and was followed, after it had become clear that this reform was a failure, by the Edict on prices and wages. Diocletian had attempted to instill public confidence in the currency by putting a stop to the production of debased gold and silver coins.

According to Kent, "Diocletian took the bull by the horns and issued a new denarius which was frankly of copper and made no pretense of being anything else; in doing this he established a new standard of value. The effect of this on prices needs no explanation; there was a readjustment upward, and very much upward."[9] The new coinage gave some stability to prices for a time, but unfortunately, the price level was still too high, in Diocletian's judgment, and he soon realized that he was faced with a new dilemma.

The principal reason for the official overvaluation of the currency, of course, was to provide the wherewithal to support the large army and massive bureaucracy — the equivalent of modern government. Diocletian's choices were to continue to mint the increasingly worthless denarius or to cut "government expenditures" and thereby reduce the requirement for minting them. In modern terminology, he could either continue to "inflate" or he could begin the process of "deflating" the economy.

Diocletian decided that deflation, reducing the costs of civil and military government, was impossible. On the other hand:

> To inflate would be equally disastrous in the long run. It was inflation that had brought the Empire to the verge of complete collapse. The reform of the currency had been aimed at checking the evil, and it was becoming painfully evident that it could not succeed in its task.[10]

It was in this seemingly desperate circumstance that Diocletian determined to continue to inflate, but to do so in a way that would, he thought, prevent the inflation from occurring. He sought to do this by simultaneously fixing the prices of goods and services and suspending the freedom of people to decide what the official currency was worth. The famous Edict of A.D. 301 was designed to accomplish this end. Its framers were very much aware of the fact that unless they could enforce a universal value for the denarius in terms of goods and services — a value that was wholly out of keeping with its actual value — the system that they had devised would collapse. Thus, the Edict was all pervasive in its coverage and the penalties prescribed, severe.

The Edict was duly proclaimed in A.D. 301 and, according to Kent, "the preamble is of some length, and is couched in language which is as difficult, obscure, and verbose as anything composed in Latin."[11] Diocletian clearly was on the defensive in announcing such a sweeping law which affected every person in the Empire every day of the week; he uses considerable rhetoric to justify his actions, rhetoric which was used before him and which, with variations, has been used in most times and places since.

> He begins by listing his many titles and then goes on to announce that: The national honor and dignity and majesty of Rome demand that the fortune of our State . . . be also faithfully administered . . . . To be sure, if any spirit of self-restraint were holding in check those practices by which the raging and boundless av-

arice is inflamed . . . peradventure there would seem to be room left for shutting our eyes and holding our peace, since the united endurance of men's minds would ameliorate this detestable enormity and pitiable condition [but since it is unlikely that this greed will restrain itself] . . . it suits us, who are the watchful parents of the whole human race, [the term "parents" refers to his associate Augustus and two Caesars] that justice step in as an arbiter in the case, in order that the long-hoped-for result, which humanity could not achieve by itself, may by the remedies which our forethought suggests, be contributed toward the general alleviation of all.[12]

In *The Common People of Ancient Rome*, Frank Abbot summarizes the essence of the Edict in the following words: "In his effort to bring prices down to what he considered a normal level, Diocletian did not content himself with half measures as we are trying in our attempts to suppress combinations in restraint of trade, but he boldly fixed the maximum prices at which beef, grain, eggs, clothing and other articles could be sold [and also the wages that all sorts of workers could receive] and prescribed the penalty of death for anyone who disposed of his wares at a higher figure."[13]

THE RESULTS OF THE EDICT

Diocletian was not a stupid man (in fact, from all accounts, he seems to have been more intelligent than all but a few of the emperors); he was therefore aware that one of the first results of his edict would be a great increase in hoarding. That is, if farmers, merchants and craftsmen could not expect to receive what they considered to be a fair price for their goods they would not put them on the market at all, but would await a change in the law (or in the dynasty). He therefore provided that "From such guilt also he too shall not be considered free, who, having goods necessary for food or usage, shall after this regulation have thought that they might be withdrawn from the market; since the penalty [namely, death] ought to be even heavier for him who causes need than for him who makes use of it contrary to the statutes."[14]

There was another clause prescribing the usual penalty for anyone who *purchased* a good at a higher price than the law allowed; again, Diocletian was well aware of the normal consequences of such attempts at economic regulation. On the other hand, in at least one respect the Edict was more enlightened (from an economic point of view) than many regulations of recent years. "In those places where goods shall manifestly abound," it declared, "the happy condition of cheap prices shall not thereby be hampered*—and ample provision is made for cheapness, if avarice is limited and curbed."[15]

---

* Those modern nations who have had to endure "Retail Price Maintenance," "Fair Trade Laws" and the various price-fixing agencies such as the International Air Transportation Association could well learn a useful lesson from Diocletian, who at least made it always legal to *lower* a price.

Parts of the price-lists have been discovered in about 30 different places, mostly in the Greek-speaking portions of the Empire. There were at least 32 schedules, covering well over a thousand individual prices or wages. The only full English translation of the Edict (done by Roland Kent) is included in the Appendix, together with a selection of some of the more interesting items, translated by Kent into U.S. equivalents as of 1920 (based upon the price of a pound of refined gold set at 50,000 denarii). The price of a bushel of barley, for instance, was set at no higher than 87 cents; beer was meant to be especially cheap, only 3 cents a quart (obviously a demagogic provision). A farm laborer was to be paid no more than $0.108 a day (most workers received their meals from their employers); masons or carpenters, however, could receive $0.217 a day.

Teachers of reading and writing could receive $0.217 per pupil monthly; teachers of Greek and Latin, $0.808 per pupil monthly. Teachers of public speaking (which prepared the way for governmental careers) were the highest paid, up to $1.08 per pupil monthly. Raw silk was almost astronomically expensive, set at $72.18 per pound—it had to be transported by land, of course, from China.[16]

The results were not surprising and from the wording of the Edict, as we have seen, not unexpected by the Emperor himself. According to a contemporary account:

> . . . then he set himself to regulate the prices of all vendible things. There was much blood shed upon very slight and trifling accounts; and the people brought provisions no more to markets, since they could not get a reasonable price for them and this increased the dearth so much, that at last after many had died by it, the law itself was set aside.[17]

It is not certain how much of the bloodshed alluded to in this passage was caused directly by the government through the promised executions and how much was caused indirectly. An historian of this period, Roland Kent, believes that much of the harm was indirect. He concludes:

> In other words, the price limits set in the Edict were not observed by the traders, in spite of the death penalty provided in the statute for its violation; would-be purchasers, finding that the prices were above the legal limit, formed mobs and wrecked the offending traders' establishments, incidentally killing the traders, though the goods were after all of but trifling value; hoarded their goods against the day when the restrictions should be removed, and the resulting scarcity of wares actually offered for sale caused an even greater increase in prices, so that what trading went on was at illegal prices, and therefore performed clandestinely.[18]

It is not known exactly how long the Edict remained in force; it is known, however, that Diocletian, citing the strain and cares of government, resulting in his poor health, abdicated four years after the statute on wages and prices was

24

promulgated. It certainly became a dead letter after the abdication of its author.

Less than four years after the currency reform associated with the Edict, the price of gold in terms of the denarius had risen 250 percent. Diocletian had failed to fool the people and had failed to suppress the ability of people to buy and sell as they saw fit. The failure of the Edict and the currency "reform" led to a return to more conventional fiscal irresponsibility and by A.D. 305 the process of currency debasement had begun again.

By the turn of the century this process had produced a two thousand percent increase in the price of gold in terms of denarii:

> These are impossible figures and simply mean that any attempt at preserving a market, let alone a mint ratio, between the bronze denarius and the pound of gold was lost. The astronomical figures of the French "assignats," the German mark after the First World War, and of the Hungarian pengo after the Second, were not unprecedented phenomena.[19] . . . Copper coins could very easily be manufactured; numismatists testify that the coins of the fourth century often bear signs of hasty and careless minting; they were thrust out into circulation in many cases without having been properly trimmed or made tolerably respectable. This hasty manipulation of the mints was just as effective as our modern printing presses, with their floods of worthless, or nearly worthless, paper money.[20]

M. Rostovtzeff, a leading Roman historian, summed up this unhappy experience in these words:

> The same expedient had often been tried before him and was often tried after him. As a temporary measure in a critical time, it might be of some use. As a general measure intended to last, it was certain to do great harm and to cause terrible bloodshed, without bringing any relief. Diocletian shared the pernicious belief of the ancient world in the omnipotence of the state, a belief which many modern theorists continue to share with him and with it.[21]

Although Diocletian's attempt to control the economy ended in complete failure and he was forced to abdicate, it was only sixty years later that his successor, Julian the Apostate, was back at the same old stand. Edward Gibbon, the brilliant historian of the period, ironically noted that:

> . . . the emperor ventured on a very dangerous and doubtful step, of fixing by legal authority, the value of corn [grain]. He enacted that, in a time of scarcity, it should be sold at a price which had seldom been known in the most plentiful years; and that his own example might strengthen his laws [he sent into the market a large quantity of his own grain at the fixed price]. The consequences might have been foreseen and were soon felt. The imperial wheat was purchased by the rich merchants; the proprietors of land, or of corn [grain] withheld from that city the accustomed

supply, and the small quantities that appeared in the market were secretly sold at an advanced and illegal price.[22]

As a desperate measure, succeeding emperors tried to tie workers to the land or to their fathers' occupations in order to prevent workers from changing jobs as a means of evading the low wages prescribed for certain professions. This, of course, was the ultimate consequence of the attempt to control wages by law.

The only legal escape for many workers was to find a willing replacement and then to give up all their goods to him. The Emperor Aurelian had previously compared a man who left his profession to a soldier who deserted on the field of battle.[23]

The historian Levy concludes his survey of the economy of the Empire by declaring that:

> State intervention and a crushing fiscal policy made the whole empire groan under the yoke; more than once, both poor men and rich prayed that the barbarians would deliver them from it. In A.D. 378, the Balkan miners went over en masse to the Visigoth invaders, and just prior to A.D. 500 the priest Salvian expressed the universal resignation to barbarian domination.[24]

FOOTNOTES

1. Levy, *op. cit.*, p. 55.

2. *Ibid.*, pp. 68–69.

3. *Ibid.*, p. 72.

4. *Ibid.*, p. 89.

5. *Ibid.*, p. 94.

6. See Roland Kent, "The Edict of Diocletian Fixing Maximum Prices," *The University of Pennsylvania Law Review*, 1920, p. 37.

7. *Ibid.*, pp. 37–38.

8. H. Michell, "The Edict of Diocletian: A Study of Price-Fixing in the Roman Empire," *The Canadian Journal of Economics and Political Science*, February 1947, p. 3.

9. Kent, *op. cit.*, p. 39.

10. Michell, *op. cit.*, p. 5.

11. Kent, *op. cit.*, p. 40.

12. *Ibid.*, pp. 41–42.

13. Frank Abbot, *The Common People of Ancient Rome* (New York: Scribner, 1911) pp. 150–151.

14. Kent, *op. cit.*, p. 44.

15. *Ibid.*, p. 43.

16. *Ibid.*, pp. 45–47.

17. L.C. F. Lactantius, *A Relation of the Death of the Primitive Persecutors*, translated by Gilbert Burnet (Amsterdam, 1697) pp. 67–68.

18. Kent, *op. cit.*, pp. 39–40.

19. Michell, *op. cit.*, p. 11.

20. *Ibid.*, p. 12.

21. M. Rostovtzeff, *The Social and Economic History of the Roman Empire* (Oxford: Oxford University Press, 1957).

22. Edward Gibbon, *The History of the Decline and Fall of the Roman Empire* (New York: Fred de Fau, 1906) Vol. 4, pp. 111–112.

23. Levy, *op. cit.*, p. 97.

24. *Ibid.*, p. 99.

New Fifty-Cent Piece

3

From Medieval to Early Modern Times

In the Middle Ages, the doctrine of the "just price" made price regulation a religious imperative. This concept, combined with the theological objection to interest (called "usury"), led to more and more economic regulation and undoubtedly was an obstacle to a rising standard of living.

Samuel Brittan and Peter Lilley in their recent book, *The Delusion of Incomes Policy*, tell us that

> Charlemagne published tables of prices at times of crop failure and an ordinance of 806 stated that "Anyone who at the time of the grain harvest or of the vintage stores up grain or wine not from necessity but from greed—for example buying a modius for two denarii and holding it until he can sell it again for four, or six or even more—we consider to be making a dishonest profit." It did not dawn on Charlemagne's advisers, any more than on contemporary politicians, that speculators can by such conduct help to reduce price fluctuations. Professor Pounds, who quotes this ordinance, conjectures that Charlemagne achieved no greater success than Diocletian had done five hundred years before.[1]

CONTROLS IN ENGLAND

In England during the Middle Ages, not only the national governments but also guilds and municipalities engaged in price-fixing as a normal activity. In the thirteenth century, officials in England "felt themselves bound to regulate every sort of economic transaction in which individual self-interest seemed to lead to injustice."[2]

In the year 1199, the government in London attempted to control the wholesale and retail price of wine. The law was difficult to enforce and eventually failed. In 1330 the passion for price-fixing stirred again and a new law was adopted requiring merchants to sell at a "reasonable" price, this figure to be based upon importation costs plus other expenses. In a few years, due to changing economic conditions, the price of wine rose far above the 1330 price and the government finally had to accept defeat once again.[3]

The many efforts to regulate the prices of wheat and bread in England came to a similar conclusion. The first attempt was apparently made in 1202; the leading law in this case was 51 Henry III which fixed precise prices for varying weights of bread. The economic historian Simon Litman notes that "The law was enforced locally on sundry occasions, but fell gradually into disuse."[4]

Antony Fisher, in his incisive book, *Must History Repeat Itself?*, discusses the events in England following the supreme tragedy of the Black Death in 1348 when about half the population perished. Obviously, a labor shortage resulted from this human catastrophe and, equally obviously, there was a tremendous rise in wages. As usual, the government, at this time controlled by the large landowners, tried to cope with this economic crisis by passing more laws. "In the thirty years after the first post-Black Death statute called 'the malice of labourers,' nearly nine thousand cases of wage enforcement were tried by the courts and in nearly all judgment was given in the employer's favor."[5] As a result of these anti-worker laws, many workers, not unnaturally, refused to sell their labor under what they regarded as unfair terms and others went from town to town trying to obtain the best wages possible. Economic dislocation followed and, as the workers became more and more angry, Wat Tyler's rebellion took place in 1381.[6]

Efforts were also made to prohibit profit-making on lending and borrowing. As far back as the eighth century, Christians were forbidden to lend money at interest, but since this religious prescription did not prevent people wishing or needing to borrow money and did not apply to other religious groups, it was natural that some Jews became bankers and money lenders.

In 1364, Edward III had the City of London pass an ordinance against usury; an Act of Parliament on the subject followed in 1390. But loopholes in the law were quickly found (as they always are) and a more stringent Act was required in 1487. This too proved worthless. It was repealed nine years later.

"During the fourteenth and fifteenth centuries," the historian W. J. Ashley tells us, "parliament and the executive left the matter [of regulation of prices, place of sale, and so on] almost entirely in the hands of the local authorities. . . . The municipal authorities frequently went beyond victuals, and regulated the prices of other articles of prime importance to the poorer classes, such as wood, coal, tallow and candles."[7]

During the reign of the Tudor family (after 1485), Parliament (under the direction of the monarch, of course) "was not content with passing acts against practices which enhanced prices. It endeavoured to fix directly a fair price not only for victuals but also for other commodities."[8] Most of these regulations received little public support anyway, principally because of their lack of effect. The Tudor age was the age of the great Tudor inflation, an inflation which was certainly precipitated by the debasement of the currency under the reign of Henry VIII. His extravagant manner of living meant that money (in the form of precious metals) had to come from somewhere. It came from the edges and the purity of his coinage.

30

A SIXTEENTH CENTURY ECONOMIST ON CONTROLS

An economist of the time, John Hales, wrote a disquisition on the problems of inflation in the Tudor period, which, except for the spelling, could have been written yesterday.

Although it was probably written in 1549 and first published in 1581, it so well illustrates the perennial principles involved that several paragraphs are quoted here (two especially pertinent passages have been italicized by the co-authors).

Many thinges coulde I here saye, and diuers forainge argumenttes coulde I make to proue it a thinge bothe honeste and necessary and behowfull to bring donne this highe price of victuall and all other thinges: but that I perceve your grace all reddy of your owine godly enclinacion muche bente vnto this purpose, for what cane be so prinsely so liberaull and so munificente a thing as to cawse that all men shall bye bothe ther victuall and all other thinges at a cheper price. *But ther is yet one other thinge which wolde helpe somewhat for the chepnes of victuall, and that is, yf neyther the lorde Mayour of London nor no other officer might haue none auctorrite to sette eney price of victuall, For vndre the Cullour of a commone wealthe they abvse ther auctorrite vnto ther owne proper Lucar. For yf eney mane do bringe eney Corne bi shippe vnto London, the Lorde Mayour hauinge eney plenty of Corne in granettes then will his Lordeshippe sette hime souche a lowe price of his Corne that he shall haue littell liste to bringe eney more vnto the Cittye. So that whan by souche means he hathe dryuen a waye all the Corne vitallers, thene he will sell his owne at what price hime selfe listeth.* Lykewise whane the Lorde Mayour dothe come into the markett and cawseth here and there a pigge to be pulled oute of a poore womans hande and to be solde by the Servauntes per chaunse vnto the Seruantes owne wife for halfe the price that it is worthe in the market or cause the Seruante to sell ij or iij baskettes full of egges for twise as maney a penney as is commonly solde in the markete: Do this eneythinge helpe the generall price of victuall? No surely, but it dothe mouche hindre it, for she that hathe by this means loste so mouche money vppon one daye: muste nedes sell a greate deall the derer at other tymes: or elles she sholde not recouer her losses, and be able to paye her rente. Lykewise the wardens of the bouchers in London: to thentent that they wolde haue but fewe bouchers to come oute of the contrye vnto the marketes in London: when they perceve eney yonge man of the Country that hathe newly sete vppe bouchers occupacon Resortinge vnto the markettes in London withe fleche, they by the Cullour of ther office and vndre pretense, that the saide fleshe is olde killid, or otherwise fawted will sell all his fleshe at halfe the price it is worthe, And thuse they will sarve hime twise or thrise vntill they haue vtterly ondon hime and dryven hime frome the Markete, or elles caused him to sell at souche highe and vn reasonable prise as the companey of

31

Bouchers in london wolde haue hime to sell at: And thuse vndre
the coulour of a Common weale they vse souche extreime tyr-
raney and Cruelnes that it wolde pitty a man's harte to be holde it:
I maruell therfor that this foresaid auctorrite is not taken a waye
frome the foresaid officers, seinge that the longe experience haue
so well declarid that the foresaid settinge of prices of victuall, do
nothing at all bringe downe the highe price thereof. But I marvell
mouche more at those men which have not only all Reddy seine the
successe of price settinge, but also the sucesse of the moste parte of
proclamacons and penaull Stattutes, and yet will holde oppinion
this present derthe of victuall may be redressid bi setting of prices
vppon victuall, but surly it is not the settinge of lowe prises that
will aney thinge a mende the matter. But it muste be the takinge
awaye of thoccation of the high prices. Yet I will not saye naye but
the Rumor therof that souche lowe prices shoulde haue bine sette
at a certen daye wollde haue donne very well, for the dought
therof wolde haue cawside maney thinges to haue fawlen some
thinge of price, And also haue cawsid maney men they shoulde
not haue letten ther groundes at so highe rente as they shoulde
elles haue donne. And also the proclayminge of souche prices at a
certen daye wolde somethinge haue quiettid the myndes of the
Commons, but now that they [*sic*, the] proclamacon shall im-
mediatly take effecte, The commonaltye shall sone perceve that it
will eyther Doo no good at all or elles mouche hurte, For yf it be
not obseruide as it is not lyke to be then dothe it non goode, and
yet it bringeth the people to a fardre disobedience. if it be so
obseruide that nothinge be solde aboue the price rated in the
proclamacion, then shall ther not halfe so mouche no nor the
forthe parte of so mouche victuall be brought vnto the market as it
was wonte to be: And what thronge and striffe is there thene lyke
to be who shall fyrste catche vppon that which commith. And what
shall thother sorte thene doo which cane gette non for no monney.
They will surly spoyle for it before the[y] famishe and though it
were a hundreth tymes proclaymede hight treason. And if it
shoulde come there vnto (god graunte they doo no worse) But
here vnto some mane will saye that ther is a good prouison in the
proclamacion if the market slake that the Justicis of peace and
other officers shall se the market fornesshede frome the farmes
nexte adioninge. But surly I thinke if the Lorde Mayour of London and all thofficers that he hathe dide nothinge elles but provide
vitall for the Cittye, yet shoulde they not be souche means provide to serve London two monthes: but that ther shoulde be
Seven tymes so muche more scacitie, then ther was yett. For how
cane hit be that they nere London which paye x *s.* or xiij *s.* iiij *d.*
for an Acre of grownde, shoulde sell ther butter by the pounde so
goode chepe, as they which dwell Seven or eyght schore myles
frome London paying not the forthe penney so muche rente for
the lyke grounde. And some grounde becase it yeldeth far better
Chise, and fare swetter and better coulorde butter thene maney

32

other groundes dothe, hathe alwaies vppon that Consideracion beine set vppon a higher rente. And some one pounde of Chise is well worth iij pounde of the moste parte of other Chise. And surely if the proclamacion be kepte ye shall neyther haue eney muttons butter or Chise solde eyther in eney Market or other where for the space of one fortenight or a monthe before mighelmas, nor like wise so longe before halloms, by cawse the Sellers will tarry so longe for the higher price, before this proclamacion the Richer sorte hade alwayes ther belly full of vitall were it neuer so deare, but the pore sorte hade maney a hongrey meall. This Proclimacon cannot bringe to passe that there shall nowe be Inoughe to serve bothe sortes. But as I said before the derthe of all thinges cannot be taken a waye in deade excepte all the cawses thereof be fyrste taken a waye, and then with outte doubte accordinge to the moste aunctiente and trewe principle in phisike: *Cessant* [sic] *causa, cesset* [sic] *effectus*.[9]

CONTROLS IN BELGIUM

In the sixteenth century misplaced economic controls were decisive in determining the fate of the most important city in what is now Belgium. From 1584 to 1585, Antwerp was besieged by Spanish forces led by the Duke of Parma who was intent on maintaining the rule of the Habsburg Empire in the Lowlands. Naturally, during a siege, food quickly becomes a scarce commodity and prices accordingly rise. The City Fathers of Antwerp reacted as many others in their position have done before and since: they passed a law fixing a maximum price for each item of food. Severe penalties were prescribed for anyone who attempted to charge the market price.

"The consequences of this policy were twofold," according to the historian John Fiske. "It was a long time before the Duke of Parma, who was besieging the city, succeeded in so blockading the Scheldt as to prevent ships laden with eatables from coming in below. Corn and preserved meats might have been hurried into the beleaguered city by thousands of tons. But no merchant would run the risk of having his ships sunk by the Duke's batteries merely for the sake of finding a market no better than many others which could be reached at no risk at all. . . . . If provisions had brought a high price in Antwerp they would have been carried thither. As it was the city, by its own stupidity, blockaded itself far more effectually than the Duke of Parma could have done."

"In the second place," Fiske concludes, "the enforced lowness of prices prevented any general retrenchment on the part of the citizens. Nobody felt it necessary to economize. So the city lived in high spirits until all at once provisions gave out. . . ."[10] In 1585 the city of Antwerp surrendered and was occupied by the forces of Spain.

A similar but even worse disaster, made more costly still by government bungling, occurred in the Indian province of Bengal in the eighteenth century. The rice crop in 1770 failed completely and fully a third of the population died. A number of scholars attribute this disaster primarily to the rigid policy of the government which was determined to keep the price of grains down rather than allow it to rise to its natural level. A price rise, of course, would have been a natural rationing system permitting the available food to be stretched out until the next harvest. Without this rationing system, the reserve supplies were quickly consumed and millions died of hunger as a direct result.

For at least once in human history, however, government did learn by experience. Ninety-six years later, the province of Bengal was again on the verge of famine. This time the procedure was completely different, as William Hunter relates:

> Far from trying to check speculation, as in 1770, the Government did all in its power to stimulate it . . . . A government which, in a season of high prices, does anything to check speculation acts about as sagely as the skipper of a wrecked vessel who should refuse to put his crew upon half rations . . . . In the earlier famine one could hardly engage in the grain trade without becoming amenable to the law. In 1866 respectable men in vast numbers went into the trade; for the Government, by publishing weekly returns of the rates in every district, rendered the traffic both easy and safe. Everyone knew where to buy grain cheapest and where to sell it dearest and food was accordingly bought from the districts which could best spare it and carried to those which most urgently needed it. [11]

The experience of Bengal, which had two failed harvests of major proportions within a century, provided a laboratory for testing the two policies. In the earlier case, price-fixing was enforced and a third of the people perished; in the latter case, the free market was allowed to function and the shortage was kept under control.

FOOTNOTES

1. Samuel Brittan and Peter Lilley, *The Delusion of Incomes Policy* (London: Temple Smith, 1977) p. 74.

2. W. J. Ashley, *An Introduction to English Economic History and Theory* (London: Longmans, 1923–5) Vol. 1, Part 1, p. 181.

3. *Ibid.*, p. 191.

4. Simon Litman, *Prices and Price Control in Great Britain and the United States During the World War* (New York: Oxford University Press, 1920) p. 6.

5. Sir Arthur Bryant, *The Fire and the Rose* (New York: Doubleday, 1966) p. 61.

6. Antony Fisher, *Must History Repeat Itself?* (London: Churchill Press, 1974) pp. 34–35. See also, Agnes Dodd, *History of Money in the British Empire and the United States* (London: Longmans, 1911).

7. W. J. Ashley, *op. cit.*, p. 30.

8. William Holdsworth, *A History of English Law* (London: Methuen, 1922–1926) Vol. 2, p. 377.

9. R. H. Tawney and E. Power, *Tudor Economic Documents* (New York: Barnes and Noble, 1963) Vol. III, pp. 338–341.

10. John Fiske, *The Unseen World and Other Essays* (Boston and New York: Houghton, Mifflin Co., 1904) p. 20.

11. Sir William Wilson Hunter, *Annals of Rural Bengal* (London: Smith, Elder, 1897) p. 7.

4

Canada and the United States:
The First Centuries

THE EARLY CANADIAN EXPERIENCE

Records from Canada are scarce before the eighteenth century, but some general comments can be made about the regulations which existed at that time.

It is certain, for example, that the internal trade of Quebec was minutely regulated. Of particular concern in the late seventeenth century were the movements of itinerant merchants; they were usually forbidden to enter into retail transactions of any sort and were subject to no less than ten general prohibitions.[1] This regulation of trade had the effect of a retail price maintenance law since the controls expressly forbade the competition of "outsiders" who, of course, threatened domestic merchants.

There is some evidence that the regulation was not an unqualified success. In 1727 the local Quebec merchants found it necessary to write to the king requesting that he suspend the operation of the itinerant merchants.[2] But this seems to have been unsuccessful as well, for a memo from the king dated April 19, 1729, contains a paragraph indicating the king's broad support for the activities of the itinerant merchants.[3]

In 1689, the Superior Council of Quebec, following the long-established European practice, gave explicit permission to municipalities to regulate the price of bread. Although the exact effect of this regulation is not known, it can be supposed that all was not well and that a change in the baker's costs would have meant a shortage of bread. Perhaps it was a situation of this sort that led to further price controls on wheat in the autumn of 1700—certainly it was clearly set down in the regulation of that year that the bakers would be required, as a result of the order, to work for the city and were constrained from working in any other way.[4]

During the 1750s, regulations were imposed upon the price of fresh codfish. But the legislators of New France had learned that imposing a set price was not enough, and the regulation explicitly forbade fishermen to refuse to sell their fish at the posted price, provided only that the buyer was solvent. Since the bulk of New France's wealth came from fishing, this was a serious law indeed, and it is significant that there was a subsequent decline in the fishery in that area as fishermen moved elsewhere.[5]

The most interesting commentary on inflation of this early period is by an unknown person writing in Quebec on April 19, 1759. The passage, which is worth reprinting here, was written as a commentary appended to an exposition of the price of commodities in Canada. The writer says:

> The excessive expense which this picture presents is such that one has perhaps never seen before an example of it. And it comes less from real scarcity than from the enormous expenditures of the government which have multiplied paper money without any consideration for the stock of commodities nor for the number of consumers. . . . The price of commodities has been rising step by step because of a similar step by step increase in the expenditures of the government. These expenditures, which one can estimate by the sum of bills of exchange, drawn on the royal treasury, have mounted as follows:
>
> in 1754 to 7 or 800 thousand livres
> in 1755 to 4,000 thousand livres
> in 1756 to 7 or 8,000 thousand livres
> in 1757 to 13 or 14,000 thousand livres
> in 1758 to 20 or 25,000 thousand livres
>
> Perhaps in this year of 1759 they will go up to 50 millions and more from whence it is easy to forsee what will be the price of commodities before January 1760. . . .[6]

THE EXPERIENCE OF THE FUTURE UNITED STATES

The early New England colonists were convinced that government ought to extend its powers into the regulation of all aspects of society, from the religious and political to the economic. "This was a defect of the age," the economic historian William Weeden tells us (though hardly a defect unique to seventeenth century Massachusetts), "but the Puritan legislator fondly believed that, once freed from the malignant influence of the ungodly, that once based upon the Bible; he could legislate prosperity and well-being for every one, rich or poor."[7]

In 1630 the General Court made a fruitless attempt to fix wage rates. Carpenters, joiners, bricklayers, lawyers and thatchers were to receive no more than two shillings a day. A fine of ten shillings was to be levied against anyone who paid or received more.[8] In addition, "no commodity should be sold at above four pence in the shilling [33 percent] more than it cost for ready money in England; oil, wine, etc., and cheese in regard to the hazard of bringing, etc., [excepted]."[9]

Weeden comments dryly that these regulations lasted about six months and were repealed.[10]

> There was an attempt at about the same time to regulate trade with the Indians. . .with the same result. The price of beaverskins [an important article of trade at the time] was set at no more than 6 shillings a skin with a "fair" profit of 30 percent plus cost of transportation. A shortage of corn, however, drove the price of that commodity up to 10 shillings "the strike," and sales of

this dwindling supply to the Indians were prohibited. "Under this pressure, beaver advanced to 10 shillings and 20 shillings per pound; "no corn, no beaver," said the natives. The Court was obliged to remove the fixed rate, and the price ruled at 20 shillings.[11]

The offshoot of the Massachusetts Bay Colony in Connecticut experienced the same artificial efforts to control prices and to divert trade from its natural courses. One nineteenth century historian has briefly summed up these attempts. "The New Haven colony," he wrote, "was made notorious by its minute inquisition into the details of buying and selling, of eating and dressing and of domestic difficulties. Then the people were mostly of one mind about the wisdom of such meddling, the community was small and homogeneous in population and religious sentiments. If such legislative interference could have been beneficient, here was a favorable opportunity. It failed utterly. The people were wise enough to see that it was a failure."[12]

The effects of controls on prices and wages were by no means confined to the English-speaking colonies in North America. In the territory that is now the State of Illinois, French settlers were faced with similar harassments from a far away government. In a history of that part of French North America, Clarence Alvord notes:

> The imposition of minute regulations issued from Versailles had been a burden upon the beaver trade. Fixed prices for beavers of every quality, that had to be bought, whatever the quantity, by the farmers at the Canadian ports, had made impossible a free development and had reduced the farmers one after another to the verge of bankruptcy. . . .An order was issued on May 26, 1696, recalling all traders and prohibiting them from going thereafter into the wilderness. . .[though] complete enforcement of the decree was impossible.[13]

THE NEW REPUBLIC TRIES OLD EXPERIMENTS

The sporadic attempts during the seventeenth and early eighteenth centuries to control the economic life of the American colonies increased in frequency with the approach of the War of Independence.

One of the first actions of the Continental Congress in 1775 was to authorize the printing of paper money—the famous "Continentals." Pelatiah Webster, who was America's first well-known economist, argued very cogently in a pamphlet published in 1776 that the new Continental currency would rapidly decline in value unless the issuance of paper notes was curbed. His advice went unheeded and, with more and more paper in circulation, consumers naturally began to bid up prices for a stock of goods that did not increase as fast as the money supply. By November 1777, commodity prices had risen 480 percent above the prewar average.[14]

39

The Congress, at least when addressing the public, professed not to believe that their paper money was close to valueless but that prices had risen mainly because of unpatriotic speculators who were enemies of the government.

On October 20, 1774, the Continental Congress decreed that "all manufactures of this country be sold at reasonable prices," and that "vendors of goods or merchandise will not take advantage of the scarcity of goods . . . but will sell the same at rates we have been respectively accustomed to do for 12 months last past."[15]

"The real causes of advancing prices," one historian notes, "were as completely overlooked by that body as they were by Lysias when prosecuting the corn-factors of Greece. As the Greek orator wholly attributed the dearness of corn to a combination among the factors, so did Congress ascribe the enormous advance in the price of things to the action of those having commodities for sale."[16]

On November 19, 1776, the General Assembly of Connecticut felt impelled to pass a series of regulations providing for maximum prices for many of the necessaries of life. It also declared that "all other necessary articles not enumerated be in reasonable accustomed proportion to the above mentioned articles."[17] Another similar act was passed in May 1777. By August 13, 1777, however, the unforeseen results of these acts became clear to the legislators and on that date both acts were repealed.[18]

In February 1778, however, the pro-regulation forces were again in the ascendancy and Connecticut adopted a new tariff of wages and prices. Retail prices were not to exceed wholesale prices by more than 25 percent plus the cost of transportation.[19] In a few months it became evident once again that these controls would work no better than the former attempts and in June 1778, the Governor of Connecticut wrote to the President of the Continental Congress that these laws, too, "had been ineffectual."[20]

The Connecticut experience, of course, was by no means unique. Massachusetts, among other states, went through almost exactly the same on-again, off-again syndrome with its own version of wage and price controls. In January 1777, a law was passed imposing "maximum prices for almost all the ordinary necessaries of life: food, fuel and wearing apparel, as well as for day labor. . . . So far as its immediate aim was concerned," an historian concludes, "the measure was a failure."[21] In June 1777, a second law was passed (a Phase II), on the ground that the prices fixed by the first law were "not adequate to the expense which will hereafter probably be incurred in procuring such articles."[22] A few months later, in September, the General Court of Massachusetts, convinced that the price-fixing measures "have been very far from answering the salutary purposes for which they were intended," completely repealed both laws.[23]

40

WASHINGTON BATTLES STARVATION

In Pennsylvania, where the main force of Washington's army was quartered in 1777, the situation was even worse. The legislature of that commonwealth decided to try a period of price control limited to those commodities needed for use by the army. The theory was that this policy would reduce the expense of supplying the army and lighten the burden of the war upon the population. The result might have been anticipated by those with some knowledge of the trials and tribulations of other states. The prices of uncontrolled goods, mostly imported, rose to record heights. Most farmers kept back their produce, refusing to sell at what they regarded as an unfair price. Some who had large families to take care of even secretly sold their food to the British who paid in gold.

After the disastrous winter at Valley Forge when Washington's army nearly starved to death (thanks largely to these well-intentioned but misdirected laws), the ill-fated experiment in price controls was finally ended. The Continental Congress on June 4, 1778, adopted the following resolution:

> Whereas. . .it hath been found by experience that limitations upon the prices of commodities are not only ineffectual for the purposes proposed, but likewise productive of very evil consequences to the great detriment of the public service and grievous oppression of individuals. . .resolved, that it be recommended to the several states to repeal or suspend all laws or resolutions within the said states respectively limiting, regulating or restraining the Price of any Article, Manufacture or Commodity.[24]

And when the controls were so removed, the repressed inflation immediately boiled out; prices rose to eighty times their pre-war level for a short period before settling down to a level just greater than the pre-war average, where they remained for the next decade.

One historian of the period tells us that after this date, commissary agents were instructed "to give the current price. . .let it be what it may, rather than that the army should suffer, which you have to supply and the intended expedition be retarded for want of it." By the fall of 1778 the army was fairly well-provided for as a direct result of this change in policy. The same historian goes on to say that "the flexibility in offering prices and successful purchasing in the country in 1778 procured needed winter supplies wanting in the previous year."[25]

The able research economist for the First National Bank of Chicago, in a recent study of controls during the Revolution, summed up the unhappy experience in these words:

> Public jawboning, private threats, ostracism, boycotts, fines— all proved useless against the flood of paper money. The price of common labor in Boston, which was fixed at three shillings a day

41

in 1777, had risen to 60 shillings by mid-1779. In April 1779, George Washington complained that "a wagon-load of money will scarcely purchase a wagon-load of provisions." In 1779, when the Continental Congress again endorsed price controls, the request was for state laws limiting wage and price increases "not to exceed twenty fold the levels of 1774." Not even that modest goal was attainable, however, and Congress allowed controls to expire when it met again in February 1780.[26]

A contemporary American economist, Pelatiah Webster, writing toward the end of the War of Independence in January 1780, evaluated in a few succinct words the sporadic record of price and wage controls in the new United States. He wrote:

> As experiment is the surest proof of the natural effects of all speculations of this kind, . . . it is strange, it is marvelous to me, that any person of common discernment, who has been acquainted with all the above-mentioned trials and effects, should entertain any idea of the expediency of trying any such methods again. . . . Trade, if let alone, will ever make its own way best, and like an irresistible river, will ever run safest, do least mischief and do most good, suffered to run without obstruction in its own natural channel.[27]

FOOTNOTES

1. "Extrait des Registres du Conseil Superieur de Quebec," *Canadian Archives*, Collection Moreau St. Mery, VI, 21 fevrier 1683, pp. 55–58.

2. *Canadian Archives*, CIIA, XLIX, 183–192 (Written about 1727).

3. "Memoire du Roi," *Canadian Archives*, Collection Moreau St. Mery, XI, pp. 332–334.

4. "Regiment du Conseil Superieur de Quebec," *Canadian Archives*, Collection Moreau St. Mery, VIII, Pt. 2, 30 mars 1701, pp. 211–214.

5. "Memoire sur le Commerce de l'isle Royale Joint a la Lettre de Monsieur Prevost," *Canadian Archives*, CIIB, XXXIII, p. 124.

6. "Exposition du Prix des Denrees en Canada: Observations," *Canadian Archives* CIIE, X, pp. 256–258.

7. William Weeden, *Economic and Social History of New England, 1620–1789* (New York, 1890) Vol. 1, p. 99.

8. *Ibid*.

9. John Winthrop, *The History of New England from 1630–1649* (Boston, 1825 and New York: Arno Press, 1972) Vol. 1, p. 116.

10. Weeden, *loc. cit*.

11. *Ibid.*, p. 98.

12. Connecticut Bureau of Labor Statistics, *Third Annual Report for Year Ending November 30, 1887* (Hartford, 1887) p. 225.

13. Clarence Alvord, *The Illinois Country, 1673–1818* (Springfield, Ill., 1920 and Chicago: Loyola University Press, 1965) pp. 106–108.

14. Anne Bezanson, *Prices and Inflation During the American Revolution* (Philadelphia: University of Pennsylvania Press, 1951) p. 35.

15. Quoted in Alan Reynolds, "A History Lesson on Inflation," *First National Bank of Chicago World Report*, July 1976.

16. Albert Bolles, *The Financial History of the United States* (New York; D. Appleton & Co., 1896) Vol. 1, p. 160.

17. Connecticut, *Public Records of the State* (Hartford, 1894) Vol. 1, p. 62.

18. *Ibid.*, p. 366.

19. William Graham Sumner, *The Financier and the Finances of the American Revolution* (New York, 1891 and New York: B. Franklin, 1970) Vol. 1, p. 65.

20. *Ibid.*, p. 66.

21. Ralph Harlow, *Economic Conditions in Massachusetts During the American Revolution* (Cambridge, Mass: J. Wilson & Son, 1918).

22. *Ibid.*

23. *Ibid.*

24. *Journal of the Continental Congress* (New York, 1908) Vol. 21, p. 569.

25. Bezanson, *op. cit.*, p. 86.

26. Reynolds, *op. cit.*

27. Pelatiah Webster, *Political Essays* (Philadelphia, 1791 and New York: B. Franklin, 1969) pp. 65–66.

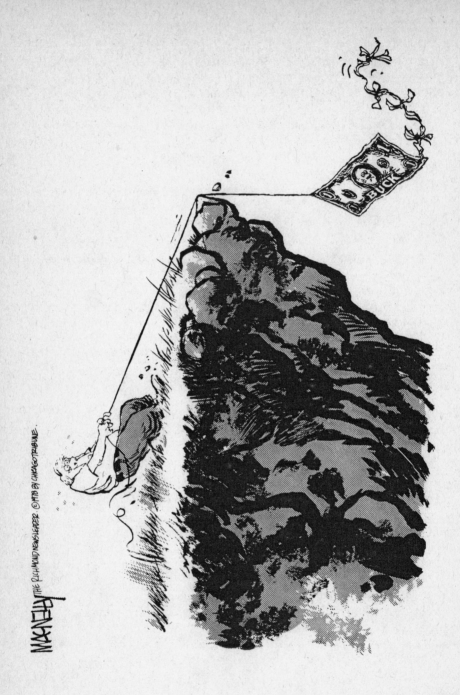

5

The French Revolution

During the twenty months between May 1793 and December 1794, the revolutionary government of the new French Republic tried almost every experiment in wage and price controls which has been attempted before or since.

At the beginning of 1793, France found itself besieged by all the powers of Europe and blockaded by the British fleet. On the home front, her currency was rapidly falling in value and inflation was rampant. On the other hand, France was the richest agricultural country in Europe and the harvest of 1793 was to be particularly abundant.[1]

Her food problem in that year was not one of production but rather of distribution.[2] A constant series of decrees and regulations, each one designed to remedy the defects of the last, had the effect of leading the bread basket of Europe to the brink of starvation.

LAW OF THE MAXIMUM

The first of these laws aimed at keeping prices down was passed by the Committee of Public Safety on May 3, 1793, together with a progressive tax on the rich and forced loans.[3] This first Law of the Maximum, as it was called, provided that the price of grain and flour in each district of France should be the average of local market prices which were in effect from January to May 1793. In addition, farmers were required to accept in payment the paper *assignats* at their face value, just as if they were coin.

Naturally many farmers kept their produce away from the markets since they were not allowed to ask a fair price for their goods in a time of rising inflation. Popular uprisings took place in several departments and by August of that year the May law was generally regarded as a dead letter.

On September 11, 1793, a new plan, which might be called Phase II, was adopted by the National Convention: a uniform price for a long list of goods was set for the whole country, with allowances made for the cost of transportation. This plan, too, was soon discarded and the Law of September 29 was proclaimed (Phase III). The new system provided that prices should be fixed at the local rates of 1790 plus one-third.

In a little over a month, this plan too was clearly shown to be a failure and the

Law of November 1 (Phase IV) was enacted. This later attempt at regulating prices was more complicated than the previous phases. Prices were to be based upon those of 1790 at the place of production, plus one-third, plus a rate per league for transportation plus 5 percent for the wholesaler and 10 percent for the retailer. Local governments were given the right to compel farmers to bring their grain to markets and to sell it at the fixed price. By the use of the army and police, enough farmers were physically transported (with their grain) to marketplaces to enable the French people to survive the last months of 1793 and the first months of 1794.[4]

The revised system of price control was, of course, no more successful than previous attempts. One scholar has succinctly explained why:

> This scheme, judged from the point of view of modern experience, had two bad features. The first was the failure to guarantee the farmer a reasonable profit, and so encourage him to put more acres under cultivation and raise larger crops. Should his labors slacken and his crops become small, no amount of energy in insisting upon a fair distribution of the product would keep the people from going hungry. The scheme not only failed to encourage the farmer, it threatened him with ruin. His expenses for tools, draft animals and wages were steadily rising, but his profits were cut down, with the prospect of further losses every succeeding month.
>
> The second blunder was the obverse of this; it was the assumption that force could be used successfully with the largest body of producing workmen the country had. The agents utilized to apply the force, when the last links in the chain of authority were reached, would be the farmers themselves, for the communal officers were either farmers or men dependent upon them.[5]

A large black market grew up all over France in response to the government's repeated attempts to control the prices of foodstuffs. Butter, eggs and meat, in particular, were sold in small quantities door-to-door, mainly to the rich. It was impossible to control this contraband trade and the net effect was to insure that the wealthy had more than enough food while the poor were left to go hungry. In other words, the actual results of the Law of the Maximum were precisely the opposite of what was intended.

THE FAILURE OF CONTROLS

An Englishwoman, living in Amiens, wrote that "Detachments of dragoons are obliged to scour the country to preserve us from famine." By the summer of 1794, demands were coming from all over the country for the immediate repeal of the law. In some towns in the south the people were so badly fed that they were collapsing in the streets from lack of nourishment. The Department of the Nord complained bitterly and with French precision that its shortages all began just after the passage of the by-now hated Law of the Maximum. They wrote to the Convention in Paris:

> Before that time, our markets were supplied, but as soon as we fixed the price of wheat and rye we saw no more of those grains. The other kinds not subject to the maximum were the only ones brought in. The deputies of the Convention ordered us to fix a maximum for all grains. We obeyed and henceforth grain of every sort disappeared from the markets. What is the inference? This, that the establishment of a maximum brings famine in the midst of abundance. What is the remedy? Abolish the maximum.[6]

The attempts of the French Republic to control the prices of food were clearly doomed; many areas of France did not wait for the national government to act but repealed the hated law by popular vote. Finally, in December 1794, the extremists in the Convention were defeated and the price control law was officially repealed. When Robespierre and his colleagues were being carried through the streets of Paris on their way to their executions, the mob jeered their last insult: "There goes the dirty Maximum!"[7]

FOOTNOTES

1. Simon Litman, *Prices and Price Control in Great Britain and the United States During the World War* (New York: Oxford University Press, 1920) p. 7.

2. Henry Bourne, "Food Control and Price-fixing in Revolutionary France," *The Journal of Political Economy*, February 1919.

3. Litman, *op. cit.*, p. 6.

4. Henry Bourne, "Maximum Prices in France," *American Historical Review*, October 1917, p. 112.

5. Bourne, *Journal of Political Economy, op. cit.*, p. 88.

6. Bourne, *Journal of Political Economy, op. cit.*, p. 93.

7. Bourne, *Journal of Political Economy*, March 1919, p. 208.

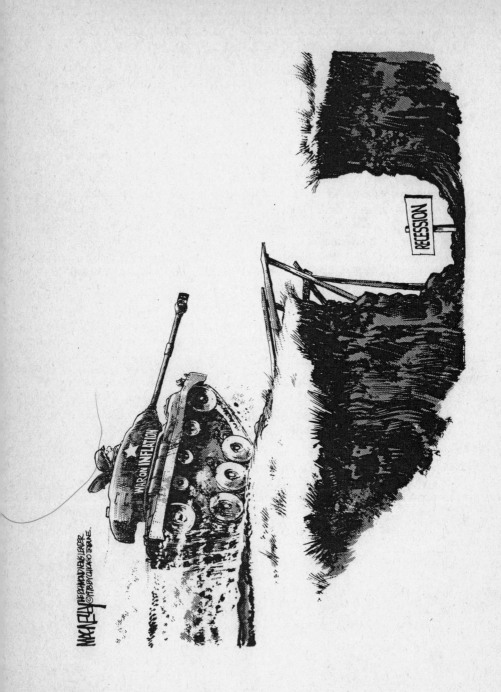

6

The Nineteenth Century:
One Success, One Failure

In the industrialized nations, at least, the nineteenth century, as we all know, was the great era of relatively free trade. For a brief period in world history, the ideas of Adam Smith were widely accepted in the most prosperous parts of the earth.

During the Victorian era, extensive wage and price controls were imposed in only a few situations, mostly during protracted wars, such as the American Civil War. In this chapter, therefore, we will briefly examine two major examples of controls in action: one famous success and one resounding failure. The success, of course, was the well-known repeal of the British Corn laws. The failure was the attempt by the Confederate States of America to, first, finance the war through inflation and, second, to restrain the inflation by price and wage controls.

THE REPEAL OF THE CORN LAWS

In Britain, one of the most spectacular reforms of the nineteenth century was the repeal of the Corn Laws, which (in the Act of 1815) prohibited or (in the 1828 Act) regulated the import of wheat and other cereal crops into the United Kingdom except when the home price was higher than a certain level. The original aim was to protect the national defense during the Napoleonic Wars (about the same time, incidentally, that an income tax of 5 percent had been brought in as a "temporary" wartime measure). The Wars had demonstrated the dangers of British reliance on foreign grain imports and were naturally supported by the landed interests which controlled Parliament at that time.

The merchants who dealt in manufactured goods resented the Corn Laws, since they worked to keep up the price of corn (wheat) and hence made living a little more expensive for workers in all sectors of the economy; this not only dampened demand for manufactured goods, but made necessary wage payments higher than would otherwise have been the case. From about 1820 onwards, the Manchester Chamber of Commerce called again and again for free trade which would enable the industrial revolution to proceed unhindered. Every year in the House of Commons, Charles Villiers moved repeal, with the support of Cobden and Bright, the famous free-traders of the time. Every year the landowners in Parliament defeated the move.[1]

When the potato crop failed in 1845, causing widespread famine in Ireland where the crop was most widely grown and consumed, import of foreign grain was allowed, and the crisis was (to some extent) alleviated. Sir Robert Peel then proposed that the Corn Laws should be repealed on a permanent basis, a move which split him and his closest supporters from the landowning classes of his Tory Party. But his move was successful and from then on, the United Kingdom enjoyed a great prosperity which could not be directly attributed to any other single source.[2]

RAMPANT INFLATION IN THE CONFEDERACY

Although, as is generally known, the nineteenth century in Europe and North America, at least, was the great era of free trade and relatively liberal government regulations, there was a notable exception to this general rule. The embattled Confederate States of America, in desperate attempts to control raging inflation, continually attempted various kinds of wage and price controls.

"The worst inflation in American history since revolutionary times," according to economic historian Eugene Lerner, "plagued the South during the Civil War. For thirty-one consecutive months, from October 1861, to March, 1864, the Confederate commodity price index rose at the average rate of 10 percent per month. In April, 1865, when Lee surrendered and the Civil War ended, the index was ninety-two times its prewar base."[3]

Why did this inflation take place? Why were Southern efforts to control it worthless? The answer boils down to the fact that the Confederate States financed the war by printing money and issuing bonds, rather than by taxation. "In the first year of the war," reports Dodd, "hardly any attempt was made to get money by internal taxation, and the blockade prevented any revenue accruing from the customs duties."[4]

There were many factors which made taxation a difficult political task. The property taxes at the start of the war were low—half a percent—and so the base for tax collection was naturally limited. Furthermore, the mechanism for collecting these taxes itself was rusty and the prospect of a conflict in the northern part of the Confederacy did not always encourage the more southern tax authorities to apply special effort in taxing their own citizens. Lerner quotes a philosophical objection to the principle of taxation stated by Governor A. B. Moore of Alabama, who was probably not alone when he declared that "The collection of this tax by the State would be an onerous and unpleasant duty, as it imposes upon the State the necessity of enforcing the laws of the Confederate government against her own citizens."[5]

And so the Confederate States, which had no experience in monetary management, made up for their naivete with considerable energy. Within five days of the Louisiana secession of January 1861, Southern forces took over the U.S. Mint at New Orleans and confiscated the bullion kept there. This formed the basis of the Confederate treasury, but "Proved to be only a tiny reserve against the billions of [dollars of] Confederate currency that were to appear during the war."[6] In September of 1862, an Act was passed to authorize note issues to any extent that would be necessary to defray public expenses, and from thence the worth of the currency started to decline rapidly. The government profited from such inflation, because it could pay off contracts made when gold was at par with notes which were already depreciating. But as the stock of money rose, so did prices, and so fell confidence in the currency.

Southern efforts to keep prices in check were largely useless against these powerful inflationary pressures. The attempts of the Confederacy to establish official prices for a wide range of commodities were foredoomed. With increasing frequency, the lists of official "fixed" prices had to be revised upward and then revised again. For example, between May 1863 and March 1865, the fixed price of bacon went from $1 per pound to $4 per pound. Beans, another staple item of diet for the boys in gray, rose from $4 per bushel to $30 per bushel.

There is no doubt that such rapid rises in food prices generated much uncertainty, insecurity and misery. Throughout the Confederacy were seen public demonstrations and riots over the price of food and other necessities. A clerk in the Department of War at Richmond recorded his observations of one such riot in 1863. Over a thousand people, mostly women, marched in procession toward the food stores, gathering carts and drays as they proceeded and then loading them with meal, flour and other provisions. It was not long before the mob took to looting nearby shops for silks, jewelry and other valuables. The troops were summoned to the scene, and the mayor of Richmond himself threatened to fire upon the rioters if they did not disperse and leave their takings. An historian quotes a description of the scene as follows:

> About this time the President [Jefferson Davis] appeared and,
> ascending a dray, spoke to the people. He urged them to return to
> their homes so that the bayonets there menacing them might be
> sent against the common enemy. He told them that such acts
> would bring famine upon them in the only form which could not
> be provided against, as it would deter people from bringing food
> to the city. He said he was willing to share his last loaf with the
> suffering people, and he trusted we would all bear our privations
> with fortitude and continue against the northern invaders, who
> were the authors of all our sufferings. He seemed deeply moved,
> and indeed it was a frightful spectacle. . . .[7]

And so price controls once again showed their ineffectiveness in dealing with price rises, but currency reform achieved much more. The Confederate Congress enacted a currency reform in 1864, which effectively reduced the stock of money in the South by one third. Later that year the general price index stopped rising and then dropped for the first time. But the success was short-lived, for as the Northern forces reduced the area of the Confederacy, Southern currency naturally made its way to the remaining Confederate States, greatly increasing the money supply in that region. As a result, of course, an unstoppable inflation showed itself on a grand scale once more.

FOOTNOTES

1. For a discussion of the corn law debate see Norman Gash, *Peel* (London: Longmans, 1976).

2. See *The Long Debate on Poverty* (London: Institute of Economic Affairs, 1973). We have already noted that British Bengal dealt with the famine of 1866 with a policy very different from its eighteenth-century one (doubtless due to the spread of free trade ideas) and attempted to facilitate speculation rather than prevent it. (See page 34.) By allowing the price of grain to rise and avoiding controls, the government in fact averted a repetition of the earlier national disaster.

3. Eugene M. Lerner, "Inflation in the Confederacy, 1861–65" in Milton Friedman (ed.), *Studies in the Quantity Theory of Money* (Chicago: University of Chicago Press, 1956) p. 163.

4. Agnes F. Dodd, *History of Money in the British Empire and the United States* (London, New York: Longmans, Green & Co., 1911) p. 304.

5. "A. B. Moore to Gentlemen of the Senate and House of Representatives, October 28, 1861," in *The War of the Rebellion*, Series IV (Washington, D.C.: U.S. War Department, 1880–1901) I, p. 698.

6. Fred Reinfeld, *The Story of Civil War Money* (New York: Sterling Publishing Company, 1959) p. 52.

7. *Ibid.*

7

The First World War

With the outbreak of the First World War in 1914 the most widespread and extensive system of economic controls in history began to go into effect. Before the war was over all the major industrialized nations had enacted regulations governing production, distribution, profits, prices and, in many cases, wages.

GREAT BRITAIN: 'WHY NOT LET IT ALONE?'

In Great Britain, the sudden and dramatic upsurge of government demands for supplies, combined with almost immediate shortages caused by the German submarine fleet, drove prices far above pre-war levels. There were insistent demands, of course, for the government to "do something."

The new government regulations, however, led to a whole series of difficulties and produced many new problems. *The Spectator* pointed out that the dangers of government controls are double in character: they are both political and economic. Politically, too much power is concentrated in the hands of the government and the people become accustomed to relying upon government to accomplish goals which can best be done by the workings of individual initiative and the free market.[1] As prices are artificially kept down in times of increasing demand and diminishing supply the only results are inconveniences and disappointments. People go to the shops expecting to find food available at the legal prices and go away disappointed.[2] Many people are also made to believe that high prices are caused by unseen manipulations which could be corrected by government manipulations.[3] They then ask for still stricter controls and yet more state interference.

Economically speaking, *The Spectator* and other journals observed that in times of increasing demands and decreasing supplies, high prices are necessary. They act as a rationing system, checking consumption and channeling goods into areas where they can be most productively used. Besides reducing waste, high prices act as a stimulant to production and importation. A free price system, in short, works to end a period of shortages and tends to solve economic problems. Government controls or rationing only act to prolong the shortages.[4] *The Fortnightly* warned that by restricting prices the government is "encouraging consumption, discouraging production and preparing disaster."[5] *The Saturday Review* declared that it is much easier to fix price ceilings than to make certain that there actually will be goods available at such prices. Once government fixes prices it is forced into the position of seeing to it that the owners of goods do not withhold them from sale and that manufacturers and farmers continue production. This amounts to nothing less than industrial conscription.[6] *The Nation* noted that without such conscription, a necessary corollary of government-fixed maximum prices set below the market rates, "a period of acute shortage, even of starvation, for the poor can be easily brought about."[7]

As *The Edinburgh Review* underscored, government regulation of the economy cannot be done without tying up the entire trade of a nation in official rules and red tape. Numerous boards and commissions must be appointed, countless clerks and supervisors employed, innumerable orders, rules and regulations must be issued. Perhaps worst of all, it also "involves endless frauds, including the wholesale forgery of food tickets, together with a general lowering of the moral standards of the community."[8] *The Fortnightly Review* remarked dryly that a process which begins with the promulgation of a few orders to hold down prices ends by reaching a stage "when practically everything is controlled, and the greater the control the more complete the confusion and the greater the economic loss."[9]

After the war, one of the most respected journals in the world, *The Economist* of London, summed up succinctly the legacy of controls in Great Britain. "Why not let it alone? [It was] repeatedly said, in response to the shortsighted demand for control of prices, that price was less important than supply, and that if the State prevented prices from rising by artificial interference, it might cut off the supplies that high prices would attract. . . . The State [nonetheless] interfered in every possible direction . . . the country now can view the results. On every side failure is visible and palpable. No single branch of trade which the government has touched shows a success."[10]

In fact, the *Economist* editorial provides an exceptionally pertinent summary of how controls actually operated in wartime Britain, and is worth quoting further.

> During the war, they [the Cabinet] had their hands full enough of war problems to satisfy a greater lust for work than any sane man ought to entertain. Yet instead of contenting themselves with dealing with the essential task of defeating our foreign foes, they persistently interfered with the course of domestic business. On each occasion the excuse put forward was that the failure to interfere would produce extravagant prices or bad distribution of supplies, or some other evil to the community which might impair the nation's war effort.
>
> . . . The blunders began from the very beginning [of price control]. For example, quite in the early days, the Home Government, judiciously pressed by Mr. Hughes, contracted to buy up all the Australian wheat at a high price, forgetting the fact that the difficulty of shipping wheat from Australia with German submarines hovering around was very much greater than getting the

same quantity of wheat from Canada or the Argentine. In the event, the Australian wheat was not shipped, and much of it has been eaten by rats. . . .

Next, the government proceeded to interfere with the coal industry; and after first passing an Act which prohibited strikes, then used its authority as a Government to concede every demand which the miners endorsed with the threat of a strike. As a result, the miners' wages were forced up far above the level of wages payable to men engaged in similar work in other industries. . . .In the same way, the State has used its power to regulate the wages of railway men, without the least regard to the economic results produced. As everybody knows, the railways are now being run at a heavy loss. . . . The excuse put forward was that increased railway rates would have been injurious to trade. The people who made that excuse were apparently incapable of understanding that it was also injurious to trade to create a deficit which would have to be met out of the taxpayers' money. . . .

After several months of this folly, the natural results began to make themselves apparent, even to the official mind. Those results included the withdrawal of the coasting steamers from the previous work of carrying heavy goods, and so relieving the railways. The steamers, with their post-war expenses, could not afford to compete with pre-war railway rates. . . .

It is, however, in the sphere of food that the Government zeal for interference has been most markedly shown, and that the Government failure has been most absolutely complete. . . . Prices are higher than they have been for many generations past, and at the same time the supply of many of our staple foods is imperilled. . . .

If this is the fine flower of achievement of the Food Ministry, with all its rules and regulations, its rationing cards, and its outpouring of millions, surely the country is justified in echoing Lord Melbourne's question: "Why not let it alone?"

LIMITED CONTROLS IN THE UNITED STATES

The experience of the United States of America with economic regulation during the war was not very different from that of Great Britain or indeed of other industrialized nations. The economic historian, Simon Litman, noted that "Government price fixing during the war was guided little by economic principles. It was not uniform either in its objects or in its methods, feeling its way from case to case. It might be termed opportunist."[11]

Oddly enough, no statute authorizing overall fixing of prices was enacted by the United States government during the war. The War Industries Board derived such power as it had to set prices from the power granted to the President to place compulsory purchase orders with any manufacturer and the related power to set priorities. In 1917 the Food and Fuel Administration was given very wide powers over the prices of food and fuel products and later the War Industries Board set up a Price Fixing Committee to establish prices for goods other than food and fuels. Generally, it fixed prices at rather high levels permitting the low-cost producers in an industry to make huge profits.[12]

In theory, the Price Fixing Committee set prices by agreement with the industry concerned. Bernard Baruch, in his 1921 report to the President on the experience of government wartime economic controls, noted that "the bases in law for different regulations were varied, and in some cases doubtful." Mr. Baruch himself later pointed out that most of the so-called "voluntary" agreements were in fact imposed on industries under the threat of commandeering.[13]

Dr. Simon Litman summed up his study of the effects of price control in the United States in 1917–18 by concluding that "The fixing of a 'reasonable' price, when the supply of a commodity is not sufficient to meet the usual demand, cannot prevent hardships and dissatisfaction. Price fixing alone does not solve the problem of keeping the poor provided with commodities; in fact, 'reasonable prices' may aggravate the situation by giving people of means an incentive and an opportunity to acquire ahead of their actual needs, thus leaving the less fortunate ones without any supply."[14]

It would be fair to conclude that most American economists regarded the experiment with price controls in the first war as having, at best, mixed results. Prices were certainly not kept down, as the figures show.

The picture from the United Kingdom is even more definite; throughout the period of the war, prices both wholesale and retail continued to rise, despite the severe restrictions put upon them.

Such was the lack of effectiveness of controls in wartime that the peaceful use of controls seemed impossible. *The American Economic Review*, in a special supplement published in March 1919, included an analysis of the possibilities of price fixing in time of peace.

> A general policy of price fixing, however democratic the government that adopts it, is an illiberal rather than a liberal policy. If we adopt a general, undiscriminating policy of price fixing as a part of a permanent peace program, we shall be going backward rather than forward; we shall be returning to a regime of authority and compulsion rather than going forward toward a regime of voluntary agreement among free citizens.[15]

CZECHOSLOVAKIA

Price controls were attempted in the first years of peace by one of the new democracies to emerge from World War I, with results similar to those predicted by British, American and other economists. A study by the Carnegie Endowment for International Peace on the economic and social history of the World War reported that "Not only did the attempt of the Government [of Czechoslovakia] to reduce prices by official order fail—it was bound to fail according to the laws of political economy—but it had the effect of constantly

56

driving prices and costs of production upwards."[16] In December of 1920, "the control of meat and fats was discontinued altogether and that of corn and flour restricted."[17] The author of this study concluded: "All this the people felt to be servitude rather than beneficent rule, so that even the most strenuous champions of economic control were compelled at length to capitulate."[18]

RUSSIA

Although price controls seemed to have been something less than efficacious in democracies, it might be expected that they would work better in a dictatorship. The case of Russia at this period provides an almost perfect laboratory. Prior to 1917, that vast country was ruled by a semifeudal despot, but after November of that year it fell into the hands of the Bolsheviks. Under the Imperial government, the bureaucracy issued contradictory and confusing regulations which only succeeded in bringing the economy to the brink of chaos. The enforcement of a consistent policy on prices was not possible mainly because the government itself violated its own rules. "The authorized agents of the Ministry of War," we are told, "bought up supplies for the army at prices much higher than those officially fixed."[19]

When the Bolsheviks seized power from the Social Democrats in November, they "abolished all freedom of trade and inaugurated a severe policy of fixed prices on all necessary articles of consumption. The peasants retaliated by refusing to sell their produce, whereupon the Soviet government began its systematic campaign against the villages, which continued for about two years and ended with the complete defeat of the Bolsheviks."[20] An observer who visited Moscow in 1919 reported that "controlled prices do not, in fact, exist. They are merely issued as decrees to which no one pays the slightest attention."[21]

It might be argued that price-fixing in the two kinds of dictatorship in Russia was still not given a fair trial because both the Czar and the communists presided over an essentially weak government ravaged by long years of war and hampered by the inherent problems of a backward nation. For a genuine test of what can be done by a firm dictatorship in a modern, industrialized nation one should examine events in Germany, the leading enemy nation.

GERMANY

"The most comprehensive experiment in Europe in direct price-fixing," according to one scholar, "was that carried out by the German government subsequent to the outbreak of war in August, 1914." After discussing all of the many regulations designed to lower prices, he concludes that the Imperial government was simply not effective in preventing a large increase in the cost of food.[22]

An English economist, writing in 1916, concluded that "the German experiment in the State control of food prices is not that maximum prices must inevitably fail in all circumstances. All that can be definitely asserted is that in this outstanding instance, Germany, the organized State *par excellence*, showed itself unable to make maximum prices work to any sort of national advantage."[23]

One of the most eminent economists of this century, the distinguished author of *Human Action* and fifteen other books, Ludwig von Mises, spent the war years in the Austrian army and had many friends in Germany. Writing a few decades later, he summed up the German experience of controls with his usual clarity and precision:

> It has been asserted again and again that German experience has proved that price control is feasible and can attain the ends sought by the government resorting to it. Nothing can be more erroneous.
>
> When the first World War broke out, the German Reich immediately adopted a policy of inflation. To prevent the inevitable outcome of inflation, a general rise in prices, it resorted simultaneously to price control. The much-glorified efficiency of the German police succeeded rather well in enforcing these price ceilings. There were no black markets. But the supply of the commodities subject to price control quickly fell. Prices did not rise. But the public was no longer in a position to purchase food, clothes and shoes. Rationing was a failure. Although the government reduced more and more the rations allotted to each individual, only a few people were fortunate enough to get all that the ration card entitled them to. In their endeavors to make the price control system work, the authorities expanded step by step the sphere of the commodities subject to price control. One branch of business after the other was centralized and put under the management of a government commissary. The government obtained full control of all vital branches of production. But even this was not enough as long as other branches of industry were left free.[24]

The record of government attempts to control the economies of the industrialized participants in the First World War, democracies and dictatorships, Allies and Central Powers, seems inescapable. In the words of a Canadian economist who examined the systems of price-fixing in Great Britain, France, Germany, the United States and Australia during this period, "The policy of fixing maximum prices. . .fails to accomplish the objects sought and it has a multitude of unforseen consequences which are frequently worse than the original evils."[25]

FOOTNOTES

1. *The Spectator*, January 23, 1917, p. 692.
2 *Ibid.*, March 31, 1917, p. 382.

3. A. Shadwell, "Food Prices and Food Supply," *The Nineteenth Century and After*, April 1917, p. 736.

4. *The Spectator*, February 6, 1915, p. 181.

5. *Fortnightly Review*, March 1917, p. 438.

6. *The Saturday Review*, September 9, 1917, p. 242.

7. *The Nation*, January 2, 1917.

8. *The Edinburgh Review*, July 1917, p. 50.

9. *Fortnightly Review*, July 1918, p. 45.

10. *The Economist*, Vol. 89, September 6, 1919, pp. 387–388.

11. Simon Litman, *Prices and Price Control in Great Britain and the United States During the World War* (New York: Oxford University Press, 1920) p. 318.

12. Struve Hensel and Richard McClung, "Profit Limitation Controls Prior to the Present War," *Law and Contemporary Problems*, Duke University, Autumn 1943, p. 195.

13. *Ibid.*, p. 196.

14. *Ibid.*, p. 319.

15. T. N. Carver, "The Possibilities of Price Fixing in Time of Peace," *American Economic Review*, March 1919, p. 247.

16. Alois Rasin, *Financial Policy of Czechoslovakia During the First Year of Its History* (New York: Carnegie Endowment for International Peace, Division of Economics and History, Economic and Social History of the World War, 1923) p. 15.

17. *Ibid.*, p. 77.

18. *Ibid.*, p. 153.

19. Kussiel Leites, *Recent Economic Developments in Russia* (edited by Harald Westergaard) (New York: Oxford University Press, 1922) p. 47.

20. *Ibid.*, p. 115.

21. S. P. Turin, "Market Prices and Controlled Prices of Food in Moscow," *Royal Statistical Society Journal*, May 1920, pp. 478–479.

22. H. L. Wilkinson, *State Regulation of Prices in Australia: A Treatise on Price Fixing and State Socialism* (Melbourne: Melville Mullen, 1917) pp. 106–116.

23. John Hilton, "Germany's Food Problem and its 'Kontrolle,' " *Nineteenth Century and After*, January 1916, p. 29.

24. Ludwig von Mises, *Inflation and Price Control* (Irvington-on-Hudson, New York: The Foundation for Economic Education, 1970) p. 6.

25. W. C. Clark, "Should Maximum Prices be Fixed?" *Queen's University Departments of History and Political and Economic Science, Bulletin* (Kingston, Ontario: Queen's University, 1918) No. 27, p. 25.

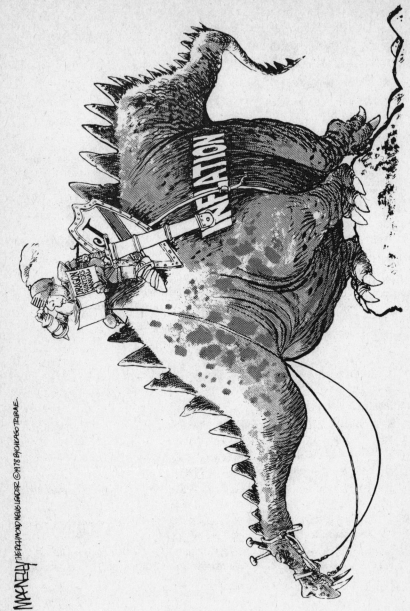

8

Three Nations Between the Wars

NEW ZEALAND

The government of New Zealand experimented quite widely with controls both during and between the two world wars. In July 1918, for example, the government of that country set down regulations for the fixing of prices (and the rationing of supplies) of gasoline. The controls were, however, short-lived and during the period of their enforcement, the supply of motor fuel was very erratic, causing serious shortage at one instant, and severe glut the next.

Milk was another target for New Zealand regulation, the controls starting during World War I. On January 18, 1917, the first Order in Council was issued, fixing the price in the Wellington area; in 1918, the Order was revised (with a higher price being enforced) and extended to cover other areas. From 1919, the Wellington City Council itself took over the administration of the milk supply.

We have seen so often that the enforcement of price regulations needs an ever-increasing bureaucracy, administering an ever-increasing set of regulations and enforcing ever-increasing penalties. New Zealand seems to be no exception. But what was the result of these controls? At the fixed price there were never adequate supplies of fresh milk in Wellington, and milk and cream were being turned to more profitable uses than human consumption. In discussing these regulations, William Sutch comments on this period that "It is noteworthy that several Wellington grocers testify that during the latter years of the war the consumption of condensed milk materially increased."[1]

Wheat was a similar victim in New Zealand. In 1914, a food commission was set up and as a result of its findings, the maximum price of wheat was fixed at 4s. 9d. per bushel and flour at Ł11 10s. per ton. This regulation was not a success, because the Commission had overlooked the fact that millers selling flour at Ł11 10s. were in fact milling at a loss. So the Commission tried again. Prices were raised to 5s. 3d. per bushel for wheat and Ł13 per ton for flour. This regulation was not a success either, because farmers refused to sell and there was no power to compel them to do so. But of course, since people needed wheat, the regulation was easily circumvented. By selling equal quantities of wheat and oats at the same time, it was easy to sell wheat at the regulation price by overcharging for the oats. Or again, wheat was sold at the regulation price and surcharges were made for the sacks, often five times their normal market price.[2]

Government control of other commodities was similarly unsuccessful; the price of sugar, for instance, rose to twice its uncontrolled price in New Zealand, even though the government took over the industry lock, stock and barrel. The (British) Royal Commission on the Sugar Supply issued its report in June 1921, in which it declared that

> The wisdom of the Government in at once taking over in 1914 responsibility for the sugar supply was in our opinion, fully proved in the sequel. But while we recognize that in the special circumstances State management was a necessity, our experience does not lead us to think that State control is a desirable thing in itself in the region of trade in commodities.[3]

They went on to say, "Our experience shows that State control of trade is not desirable. For successful trading, constant vigilance, quickness of decision and secrecy are wanted, which is difficult to secure in a public department."

The British have a tradition of understatement.

JAPAN CONTROLS SILK PRICES

At various times since the Great War, Japan attempted to control prices in the silk market. In 1930 the Silk Stabilization and Indemnification Act was passed, probably the most sweeping legislation of this period. The method of price control deployed was the adjustment of supply; the government withheld surplus stocks from the market and made it easier to export silk from the country. Finally, in a move which displays the real senselessness of price controls, the Japanese authorities attempted to limit the production of silk—one of the country's major exports.

Provincial magistrates, upon whom the burden of the execution of these controls devolved, did not seem to exert much effort to achieve success. They knew that their local constituents would not put up with such high-handed government interference.

The futility of the measure is indicated by the fact that although from March to June 1930, the government took 143,000 boxes of silk out of the market, the price of silk still fell in price from 1,100 yen to 850 yen. So much for price stabilization through the management of supply.[4]

CONTROLS FAIL IN BRAZIL

The South American continent is not without experience of price regulation. Brazil flirted with coffee price-fixing between 1924 and 1931, and the scheme was retrospectively declared to be an utter flop, and its failure precipitated a change of government in that country.

Various tools were constructed: a control of exports, the regulation of shipments, open market purchases and loans to planters who would keep supplies deposited in government regulatory warehouses. The government sought to keep prices stable by such regulation of supply. But what they found was that government warehouses contained ever-increasing quantities of coffee, while prices were not all that stable. The cost of accumulating and keeping these huge supplies was so high that Brazil had to negotiate large international loans —$50,000,000 in 1926, and another $25,000,000 in 1929, and finally $100,000,000 in 1930. But even these loans were insufficient to enable them to carry the large supplies of coffee which continued to mount up.[5]

The controls broke down completely in 1931 and huge amounts of coffee had to be destroyed over the following seasons.

Not only large crops, but the effects of price-control itself outflanked the Brazilian government. The relatively high price of Brazilian coffee encouraged coffee demand to seek satisfaction in other countries and as demand dwindled, the government had to impound more and more coffee to keep the price up. Furthermore, the guaranteed price which the government offered encouraged further planting of coffee crops, adding even more to the supply. As Jules Backman comments, "The increase in supplies, as a result of the above-mentioned combination of factors, accompanied by a stationary or decreasing demand could have only one effect so far as the outcome of the scheme was concerned, and that was failure."[6]

FOOTNOTES

1. William Ball Sutch, *Price Fixing in New Zealand* (New York: Columbia University Press, 1932) p. 130.

2. *Ibid.*, Chapter VI, *passim*.

3. *Final Report of the Royal Commission on the Sugar Supply* (London: Her Majesty's Stationery Office, 1921).

4. Jules Backman, *Adventures in Price Fixing* (Menasha, Wisconsin: Farrar & Rinehart, 1936) Chapter VI.

5. *Ibid.*, Chapter IV.

6. *Ibid.*, p. 23.

9

National Socialist Germany

To the modern observer the most striking characteristic of Nazi Germany's wage and price controls is the iron rigidity of their enforcement and their elaborate nature by comparison with what the world had seen before and much that it has seen since. Both these characteristics are only fully explicable when they are examined in the context of the time and the system which imposed them. To the Nazis, wage and price controls were not an unpleasant cure for a temporary problem of inflation which could be dispensed with as soon as the system was able to function normally again, as they are to many democratically oriented policymakers today. They were an integral and permanent part of the collectivist economic system designed to last for the lifetime of the Reich. The tasks they performed were essential in Hitler's whole game plan (enunciated in *Mein Kampf*) "to secure for the German people the soil . . . on which future generations of German peasant stock will be able to rear mighty sons. . . ."

In other words, from 1926,* Hitler had intended to build up Germany as a war economy—his aim was not to depend on any form of market-oriented economic order for this would never have allowed the Nazis to marshal the activities of the population towards the building up of the German war machine to the extent that only centrally directed planning could.

The common characteristic of all war economies in modern times has been the

---

*Fascist Italy had already moved toward government control over the economy as soon as Benito Mussolini was installed as Prime Minister and "Duce" in 1922.

On April 3, 1926, the Rocco Law of Corporations was promulgated under which 22 "Corporazione" were established to be presided over by Mussolini. The Labor Charter of April 21, 1927, included a section (Article IX) which specifically allowed the government to intervene in all economic affairs. "State intervention in economic production," it declared, "takes place only when private initiative is lacking or insufficient, or when the state's political interests are at stake. Such intervention may take the form of controls, encouragement or direct management." See Shephard Clough and Salvatore Saladino, *A History of Modern Italy* (New York: Columbia University Press, 1968) p. 467.

The provisions of this law were soon put into effect in an attempt to stem the tide of the worldwide depression. Despite rigid price-fixing backed by a totalitarian regime, Italian prices and wages steadily declined and many businesses collapsed as the unemployment rolls swelled. Although the economy still floundered, government controls did have at least one major result—they gave Mussolini almost absolute control over the labor movement and slightly less control over industry.

high proportion of the GNP consumed by the government. To finance these purchases, the government will invariably, in a war, choose the method of payment which imposes as little cost as possible upon itself. This usually means that in practice the government "prints money" to pay for its purchases and thereby runs a risk of inflation since productive resources are likely to be in a prolonged state of excess demand. To overcome this, rationing has frequently been the most favored means of resource allocation because this allows the government to effectively arrogate to itself those resources available that it wants for the war effort. All of these methods, wage and price controls, inflationary financing, and rationing, were pursued in Nazi Germany.

Although the Nazis went a great way to meet the problems that had occurred in the First World War, this did not prevent the classical weaknesses and side effects of wage and price controls occurring and worsening as time went on. As economic theory predicts, goods were withdrawn from the market, quality reductions occurred, black markets appeared and barter began to take the place of previously all-cash transactions.

However, one of the little known facets of Nazi economic totalitarianism which explains the speed with which the German economy responded to Nazi planning measures is that so much of the elaborate superstructure that the Nazis required for successful policy implementation was already existent and available for that use. More explicitly, the cartelization of the economy, state control of the banks, ownership of a sizable fraction of industry, regulation of many aspects of business activity, incorporation of labor into organized units with central control working closely with government and intervention in foreign trade— all existed before Hitler. And this had not come about by means of Nazi legislation. It had arisen under the social democrats who had held power since the birth of the ill-fated Weimar Republic. Two historical considerations bear acutely on our understanding of what happened under Hitler.

Firstly, some of this state control had come about as a result of deliberate policy design, for example, the legislation establishing organized mediation and shop councils which placed trade unions at the dead center of any industrial policy. Other controls came about by way of the exigencies of the short-term situation, for example, the nationalization of the banks after the 1931 banking crisis.

Secondly, the social democrats, however these levers of power had come to them in the first place, had never intended to use them in any way resembling the inhumanity of the Nazis. The problem was that the other side of the equation, how to ensure that nobody of evil intentions got into a position to use these controls, was not dealt with at the time.[1]

It is thus essential, if one wishes to understand what happened under the Nazis, to briefly review economic history under the Weimar Republic.

WEIMAR GERMANY'S GREAT INFLATION

The Great Inflation of post-World War I Germany was one of the most significant events of this century, since it was one of the main factors, and possibly *the* principal factor, that led to the rise of Adolph Hitler.

Currency in circulation rose from 6 billion marks in 1913 to 92,000,000,000,000,000 marks in November 1923.[2] In his book, *The Great Inflation: Germany 1919–1923*, William Guttman tells how a cup of coffee rose in price from 5,000 marks to 8,000 marks while he was drinking it. A pair of shoes costing 12 marks in 1913 was selling for 32 trillion marks in November 1923.[3]

One of the most pointed commentaries on this social upheaval was written by the distinguished German author, Thomas Mann.

> A severe inflation is the worst kind of revolution. The stern measures—currency restrictions, curtailed production, draconic taxes—that a government can and sometimes must take systematically are nothing by comparison. For there is neither system nor justice in the expropriation and redistribution of property resulting from inflation. A cynical 'each man for himself' becomes the rule of life. But only the most powerful, the most resourceful and unscrupulous, the hyenas of economic life, can come through unscathed. The great mass of those who put their trust in the traditional order, the innocent and unworldly, all those who do productive and useful work, but don't know how to manipulate money, the elderly who hoped to live on what they earned in the past—all these are doomed to suffer. An experience of this kind poisons the morale of a nation.
>
> A straight line runs from the madness of the German Inflation to the madness of the Third Reich. Just as the Germans saw their marks inflated into millions and billions and in the end bursting, so they were later to see their state inflated into 'the *Reich* of all the Germans', 'the German Living Space', 'the New Europe', and 'the New World Order', and so too they will see it burst. In those days the market woman who without batting an eyelash demanded a hundred million for an egg, lost the capacity for surprise. And nothing that has happened since has been insane or cruel enough to surprise her.
>
> It was during the inflation that the Germans forgot how to rely on themselves as individuals and learned to expect everything from 'politics', from the 'state', from 'destiny'. They learned to look on life as a wild adventure, the outcome of which depended not on their own effort but on sinister, mysterious forces. The millions who were then robbed of their wages and savings became the 'masses' with whom Dr. Goebbels was to operate.
>
> Inflation is a tragedy that makes a whole people cynical, hard-hearted and indifferent. Having been robbed, the Germans became a nation of robbers.[4]

After the worst of the inflation declined, Germany was still in severe economic difficulties. Germany relied heavily on exports to pay war reparations and was hit more seriously than most following the world slump of 1929. Although economic recovery from the defeat of the First World War had been remarkable, Germany was not as economically strong nor as politically mature as Britain, the U.S., or France. From 1929 unemployment rose rapidly, reaching 6 million in 1932 (the worst year of the world slump for both Germany and the U.S.). The surprising fact, however, was that the organized unions were so strong despite the slump. This resulted from ten years of legislation from 1918 which was intended to "enhance the unions' scope, strength, and authority."[5] These laws included a system of mediation and arbitration whereby bargaining was between trade unions and employers or employers' organizations; this system was sanctified in law as the most desirable and normal system of labor relations. The corollary of this practice was that company unions or independent associations of shop floor workers were excluded from recognition. Furthermore, individual workers were forbidden to make their own contracts with management and if they lost union membership they were not allowed to continue working in their jobs.

Official arbitration agencies tried to resolve points of dispute between employers and unions when agreements could not be reached. After a time the government involvement increased. It arrogated to itself the power to declare an agreement "generally binding" whereby an agreement made for one firm in a district could be extended, by decree, to all those in the district in the same industry. This immensely increased the power of the unions who would select the financially strongest firm in a district and use this one to set a standard which poorer employers were forced to accept. However, this still left instances where agreement was not reached and a dispute became protracted. To solve this problem, the government announced that the mediator could state his own decision and, providing one of the parties to the dispute accepted it, declare it to be the going wage. While this instrument was used only exceptionally at the start, it soon became the rule; large sectors of the Weimar Republic's industry therefore came to acquire politically determined wages. Hence, by subterfuge rather than design, a crude kind of wage control came into existence and the government was inextricably entangled in many industrial wage conflicts.

The government apparatus also had a firm grip on the agricultural markets by the time Hitler came to power in January 1933. The world slump of 1929 meant that there was great pressure on agricultural prices which threatened to put many German farmers out of business. In particular, the rye farms of north and northeast Germany were badly hurt and very soon the government was committed to a tangled web of staggered import duties, import quotas, embargoes, government stockpiling, a government monopoly of corn, and a host of minor controls.

The slump of 1929 also severely weakened the German banking system. What caused its total collapse was, firstly, the massive increase in Nazi votes in the September 1930 elections which increased their representation in the Reichstag from 12 to 107 and, secondly, the Austrian banking crisis in 1931. These two events led to a massive withdrawal of foreign deposits from German banks and led to the collapse of one of the four largest banks. This in turn caused a panic throughout the whole German banking system and led to the government declaring a bank holiday that was only subsequently lifted over a period of several weeks. This "rescue" of the banking system then took the form of the government-controlled banks giving funds in exchange for newly-issued bank equity—the old equity being written down to a nominal value.

Thus, in the words of Gustav Stolper, "It is an historic fact that deserves close attention that the German banking system had thus been virtually nationalized by the Republican government on the very eve of the National Socialist revolution."[6]

Another important feature of the German economy before the Nazis was the high degree of cartelization. When Chancellor Brüning began his severe deflation in 1930–31, the controls over the cartels were used as a major policy tool to lower prices. This was one more way in which government administration replaced the market before the Nazis achieved power.

THE NAZIS COME TO POWER

As we pointed out earlier, Nazi price control was more rigorous and elaborate than anything seen earlier in Germany or in any other nation.[7]

Germany had seen some degree of price administration in the latter days of the Weimar Republic. The Nazis drew upon this experience and also upon the price freeze enforced during the First World War. These two precedents conditioned many of the initial features of the policy followed from 1936.

There were essentially two identifiable periods of Nazi price control. The first, from 1933–36, was the period in which the administrative bureaucracy and enforcement mechanisms were still in their evolutionary stages. The second period was from 1936 onwards when a full-fledged framework embodying war economy regulations was in force in Nazi Germany. Although this apparatus was readily modified in the light of the exigencies imposed by the war, it remained, in conceptual terms, essentially the same until the downfall of the Reich.

In the first period, the powers available to the Reich Price Commissioner were used to the full and extended further on several occasions. Three decrees in 1934 made it illegal to increase prices or to change customary payment periods or discounts/credits. Punishment was an unlimited fine and/or a prison sentence. Further decrees in the same year compelled all cartels and trade associations to file full lists of their administered prices with the Price Commissioner.

In the case of prices which were not traditionally administered, the government fixed either maximum prices or maximum and minimum prices, although some of the less important prices were left to float. In certain areas, such as

69

nonprecious metals, meats and sausages and textiles, the government decree demanded that prices be frozen at a preexisting level.

An earlier system of administration and supervision by several agencies was replaced, on December 14, 1936, by a single, centralized authority controlling all prices. However, prices still continued to rise and control was decentralized once more.

One great problem for the Nazis was the control of import prices. On September 22, 1934, a decree was issued which allowed increases in the prices of imported commodities or commodities containing imports whose prices could rise by the relevant weighted proportion. Nevertheless, this was not to prove to be a liberalization of price control, because it was also stated that in no case should the price of any imported commodity be higher than its price in any foreign market that day. Thus, it appears that the Nazis had to admit that even they could not suspend all the laws of economics.

The dividing line between the first and second phases of price control was marked by the creation of the New Office of Price Formation. This spawned a large number of local offices and increased the state price-fixing bureaucracy considerably. It also ushered in the concept of the "just price" for a commodity. This was defined as the price which served the following government objectives:

1) helped to build up the equipment necessary to the execution of the second Four-Year Plan;
2) helped to secure production of the so-called Four-Year Plan commodities;
3) contributed to the production of a sufficient quantity of consumer commodities.

The Reich Price Commissioner was the final arbiter of whether a price was "just."[8]

It is interesting to note that a price was certainly not "just" if:

1) it would result in "cut-throat" competition;
2) it would yield an above normal profit to the producer.

("Normal" was defined as the rate of return on long-term federal bonds.)

The "Price Stop" of November 26, 1936, froze all prices (both free and administered) at their October 17th levels. It was clearly a measure conceived in the light of experience from the First World War. It was retrospective and unannounced, thus preventing anticipation and consequent advance price raising. Besides freezing all prices, including credit terms, discounts, and so forth, at their prevailing levels, it also meant that the producers selling the same product at different prices found those prices frozen with the difference intact.

This mechanism, the price stop, was extremely effective in destroying the whole market system and price determination of production decisions. As such, the Nazis used it to centrally plan the economy with great effect. Punishment for evasion was an unlimited fine or prison sentence.

The price stop was followed by about seven thousand decrees directing the alteration of individual prices. Sometimes, these decrees permitted sought-after increases to businessmen; others compelled a reduction.

There were also decrees which fixed maximums and/or minimums and which fixed margins and rebates. The only items for which flexible prices were permitted were imports on which Germany was crucially dependent.

In order to control wages, the Nazis dealt with the comparatively powerful trade union movement very quickly after obtaining power. The annual May Day parade was usually a day of demonstrations by organized labor and socialist parties, but Dr. Goebbels' sophisticated propaganda machine turned it into a day for Nazism. Goebbels read a proclamation in which he said that it would be a day to "affirm life's values of courage, work, and national labor."

On May 2, 1933, Hitler's storm troopers closed all trade union offices, seized all union leaders, and formed the *Deutsche Arbeitsfront* (German Labor Front). This was to be a compulsory national labor organization, including all managers and professionals; it was a puppet, of course, of the Nazi Party. Wages were thus administered according to a national plan.[9] They hardly rose from 1933. Workers now no longer had freedom of movement, although the slightest behaviorial deviation could cost a worker his or her job. Workers became "followers" and managers "leaders" in the official propaganda. Unemployment insurance still took 6 percent of the wage packet even after unemployment had been (officially) abolished. The Labor Front organized workplace oriented outings and holidays, sports, theater, and other approved forms of rest and recreation. In essence, the worker became a serf.

The system of rigid wage and price control continued, amended from time to time as the situation warranted, throughout the war. (It even remained in force for three years afterwards under the Allied Occupation.)

DID NAZI CONTROLS WORK?

More interesting, however, is the fact that even this rigid structure could not prevent all of the problems associated with wage and price controls that basic economic theory would predict.

When Hitler imposed the price stop in 1936, he froze the n-dimensional constellation of related prices in a unique and arbitrary historical pattern. For, while the underlying determinants of economic parameters (such as tastes, weather, time itself, the state of the war, foreign prices, and so forth) were all changing continually, the economy of Germany had been suspended. No longer did prices perform their crucial role as signals of discrepancies between supply and demand which would be corrected by entrepreneurs altering their plans to meet unforeseen needs. Yet, the Nazis needed to finance their impending war and for this they returned to the orthodox method of printing money. Horst Menderhausen (Assistant Chief of Price Control, U.S. Military Government of Germany, 1947–48) estimates that by 1947 currency in circulation in the four zones of Germany and Berlin was approximately ten times the amount that circulated in the Reich before Hitler imposed the price stop in 1936. In 1944 the increase from 1936 had been fivefold, whereas industrial production had only increased by 36 percent.[10] The official price index rose by only 7 percent between 1936 and 1944. By comparison British prices rose 76 percent in the same period and by 22 percent between 1940 and 1944. However, there is good evidence to show that real prices doubled between 1937 and 1944, the difference being manifested, as usual, through product changes, quality reductions and black markets.

Product changes certainly occurred as the economy moved onto a war footing. This gave firms the chance to introduce new items and obtain better prices than they did for their previous line of goods. This was certainly one way in which firms raised prices even though it meant going through a cumbersome and bureaucratic price fixing procedure.

Quality reductions are an old and well-known method of raising prices in a time of controls. It was practiced by the rulers of England (and, indeed, of Egypt) in the production of coins from precious metals long before the Nazi era. The Nazis had explicitly banned quality reduction as an evasion of the original Price Stop decree, and it is perhaps a measure of how helpless they knew they were to enforce it that they proscribed such heavy penalties for violators who were caught.

The presence of a large black market in Nazi Germany is widely documented.[11] It consisted mainly of transactions in finished products and prices varied from place to place. The existence of the black market is more evidence that men can never banish the marketplace entirely by planning; they can only make it unofficial. In Nazi Germany, as elsewhere, the black market played a crucial role in absorbing excess money. It appears that at times during the war years, prices were so high and such was the scarcity of goods that a fairly small volume of transactions would absorb a large amount of income.

Another variety of evasion of controls which appeared, as predicted, in Nazi Germany was bilateral exchange (barter). For the vast majority of transactions however, it was extremely inefficient in terms of search costs and price equilibration compared with money. Still, it was a method by which people could satisfy wants.

The crucial point is that, despite iron controls, inflation was *not* halted in Nazi Germany, just as we shall see it was not halted in the U.S.S.R.; it was simply changed in form. The government had sufficient power to enforce, for the most part, a ban on explicit price rises and hence these were replaced by longer queues for the product which was in deficient supply. The choice, if the money supply is expanded in excess of real output, is higher prices or larger queues. At least, the saving grace of the market is its subtle genius in reacting to a deficiency in such a way as to produce negative feedback and thereby bring forth greater output in the process.

In Nazi Germany all of the above evasions occurred because price rises, and hence greater output, were only being permitted in those industries where such a result concurred with the government's sense of priorities. The market, by way of contrast, allows different hierarchies of values to contend concurrently.

Needless to say, even the reputed Nazi efficiency was not perfect and frequent miscoordinations of plans (what GIs called "SNAFUs") prevailed. One example, recounted by Brittan and Lilley, is particularly revealing. A circular in 1943 said that tanks had priority over packing cases, but at that time dozens of completed tanks could not be dispatched—there were no packing cases because of a nail and screw shortage. The essential problem is dealt with in detail by Walter Eucken. In 1948, he wrote:

> In the centrally administered economy, there is quite another relationship between needs and supplies. The tension between the two finds no effective expression in the markets. Demand and supply for iron, coal, and all other goods does not originate with different independent economic individuals, each with his own plans. Rather, the fixing of needs and the direction of production is in a single hand. The planning authorities consequently proceed by first fixing the requirements for coal, bread, houses, and so on, and then adjusting the productive process to these needs by their aggregate valuations and production orders. But they do not have to proceed like this. They can also proceed subsequently by altering the consumption side of the equation, which is then adjusted to the production side. Allocations of textile goods can suddenly be cut or the construction of a new factory halted. Consumers cannot control the central administration. All economic power is concentrated in the central administration, which is thus itself subject to no controlling mechanism.
>
> Perhaps this may be regarded as a weak point in the centrally administered economy. In fact, it is only a weak point if the maximum satisfaction of needs is regarded as the purpose of production.[12]

At the end of the war, an authoritative critique of the Third Reich's economic policy was given by Herman Goering (who was responsible, among other things, for economic planning) while a prisoner of war in 1946. He told the war correspondent, Henry J. Taylor, that

> Your America is doing many things in the economic field which we found out caused us so much trouble. You are trying to control people's wages and prices—people's work. If you do that you must control people's lives. And no country can do that part way. I tried it and failed. Nor can any country do it all the way either. I tried that too and it failed. You are no better planners than we. I should think your economists would read what happened here. . . .
>
> Will it be as it always has been that countries will not learn from the mistakes of others and will continue to make the mistakes of others all over again and again?[13]

Finally, it is instructive to note that price control in Germany was not ended until 1948, and even then it was done without the consent of the Allied Military Government. Professor Ludwig Erhard, the West German Economics Minister (and future chancellor), made the announcement on a *Sunday*, precisely because the allied bureaucracy was at home and the measure could have the desired effect before they could get together and tell each other that it could not be done. This, of course, was the beginning of the German economic "miracle."

FOOTNOTES

1. See F. A. Hayek's classic chapter, "Why the Worst Get on Top," in his book, *The Road to Serfdom* (Chicago: University of Chicago Press, 1967).

2. Michael Jefferson, *et. al.*, *Inflation* (London: John Calder, 1977) p. 44.

3. William Guttmann and Patricia Meehan, *The Great Inflation: Germany, 1919–1923* (Hampshire, England: Saxon House, 1975) p. 61.

4. Michael Jefferson, *op. cit.*, p. 166. This article by Thomas Mann was published under the title "The Witches Sabbath" in *Encounter*, February 1975.

5. G. Stolper, *The German Economy: 1870 to the Present* (London: Weidenfield and Nicholson, 1966).

6. *Ibid.*

7. According to *The Nazi Economic System*, by Otto Nathan (Durham, N. C.: Duke University Press, 1944, p. 216), "Price control was the entering wedge and before long it became one of the basic instruments of total economic control. The entrepreneur continued to be the owner . . . but the cost accounting system which was imposed upon him, in connection with price control, enabled the government to supervise and control minute aspects of the enterprise and every single move the entrepreneur made."

8. The Commissioner of Price Formation was described as an official who no longer merely watched over prices. "He was supreme arbiter. He made and unmade them." One of the holders of this office wrote in 1940 that "If the government wants to establish prices it can succeed only if the price-setting agency secures supreme power. No doubt such an objective will not be welcomed by many; but power is necessary if one wants to maintain the price level as stable as possible." See Otto Nathan, *op. cit.*, p. 225 and p. 236.

9. The Law Regulating National Labor was enacted on January 20, 1934. Wages were determined by labor trustees, appointed by the Nazi-controlled Labor Front. Hitler was quite clear about his plans to keep wages low. "It has been the iron principle of National Socialist leadership," he announced, ". . . not to permit any rise in the hourly wage rates but to raise income solely by increase in performance." See William Shirer, *The Rise and Fall of the Third Reich* (New York: Simon and Schuster, 1960) p. 263.

10. Stolper, *op. cit.*, p. 142 and p. 162.

11. See, for instance, H. Menderhausen, "Prices, Money and Distribution of Goods in Post-War Germany," *American Economic Review*, June 1949; and Samuel Brittan and Peter Lilley, *The Delusion of Incomes Policy*, Chapter 4, "Totalitarian Incomes Policies" (London: Temple Smith, 1977).

12. Walter Eucken, "Theory of the Centrally Administered Economy," *Economica*, May 1948.

13. Quoted in F. A. Harper, *Stand-by Controls* (Irvington-on-Hudson, N.Y.: Foundation for Economic Education, 1953) p. 20.

10

The Soviet Union

The Soviet Union today presents the best example of a mature and long-lived total wage and price control policy in operation. Its planned economy has been almost totally rigid in its opposition to any form of price structure ever since the end of Lenin's "New Economic Policy" in the 1920s.

Stalin's place in history as one of the most ruthless leaders of all time was partly due to the measures he took to regulate the economy. Because the Soviet Union is a totally planned economy, the policy goals are whatever the planners say they are since ultimately the power of the state is always sufficient and ready to infringe any individual right and inflict any amount of coercion on citizens to ensure that the central plan is fulfilled. Some idea of the nature of the task of regulating the Soviet economy can be gleaned from the fact that there are over ten million separate prices in the Soviet plan. Whereas the success of a Western economy would naturally be judged on its ability to satisfy consumer wants, in the Soviet Union, as in any centrally planned economy, low marks would be gained by this test since the purpose of central planning is not to satisfy consumer desires. It can only fulfill itself in terms of its own prescribed parameters (that is, the goals of the planners).

A. S. Shkurko,[1] Deputy Director of the Labor Research Institute, has provided a very lucid account of the current Soviet wage system and the historical circumstances that led to it. The Soviet state fixes wages in two ways. In the first place, it sets for each enterprise the total wage bill for the year. Secondly, it sets the national weekly wages for every kind of job. Factory or office managers have some flexibility since they have included in their wage fund a sum for bonus payments and there is evidence that this is used to create a more realistic wage structure than the central planners originally designed. Every factory has an output target allotted to it by the planning authority; in theory this should rise at the same rate as the long-term rise in productivity to keep wages constant. In practice, in order to obtain sufficient skilled labor, the target will be increased less than estimated productivity so that workers find it easier to "over-fulfill" plans. For this "glorious socialist achievement" they are entitled to bonus payments and hence their effective earnings are somewhat above the state's official level.[2]

77

IS THERE A SOVIET LABOR MARKET?

One question that has been contested in the West is whether there is a labor *market* of any sort in the U.S.S.R.

Brittan and Lilley point out that Stalin's strict anti-mobility laws of the 1940s were relaxed in 1956 and that new workers are, within a limited field, allowed to change their jobs.

Peter Wiles[3] has stated that the Soviet factory manager faces a competitive labor market, perhaps the only "official" competitive market in the Soviet Union; managers were given the power to hire, fire, and reallocate the wage fund in 1965. Thus, in practice, managers have, in the absence of free trade unions, enormous power to get rid of unskilled or otherwise unsatisfactory workers and to pay semi-disguised perks to better workers. However, Wiles qualifies this statement by adding that this power has in fact been used only rarely and kept under the strictest Party control.

If Wiles' original assertion is correct, then the ironical result is that labor is the official "residual" that is forced to adjust to the State's other goals and not (as advocates of workers' states would have it) the other way around.

If his latter quasi-retraction is correct, then a skeptic of the virtues of Soviet communism would conclude that in practice, labor is the "residual."

Returning to the central features of central planning in the macroeconomic sense, the output of various commodities is decided upon on the basis of previous outputs and stock figures at the time a new plan is drawn up. This naturally leads to a fundamental question in the debate between pricing and planning generally: is there repressed inflation in the Soviet Union? In other words, do price controls eliminate inflation in the Soviet Union or are they a failure there also?

Michael Jefferson notes, in *Inflation*, that the cost of living of the Soviet urban industrial worker seems to have gone up by 65 percent between 1927 and 1937 while real wages went down by about 50 percent. These price rises occurred despite the price falls promised in several successive Five Year Plans; they seem to have been due to a large increase in short-term credit and currency provided by the State Bank in the decade of the 1930s. The currency expanded about eight times in the period 1929–1941.[4]

Advocates of the repressed inflation position point to the continued existence of widespread queuing[5] and a whole "parallel economy" of backhanders, illegal trading, smuggling, theft, and so on, which has existed for a long period of time and become institutionalized to the extent that virtually *every single Soviet citizen is involved*.[6]

THE BLACK MARKET

Many Westerners think that the black market is limited to higher quality Western clothing. However, Simes shows that this is only one minor part of a whole parallel market. In fact, for automobile service, high quality foods, repairs on apartments and virtually any personal service, extra payments are the way to ensure prompt and efficient attention. For retailers, regular deliveries of the best stock can only be assured by backhanders to suppliers and at the production stage hidden additional wages are provided to retain good workers.

The attitude of the authorities to this is that it is formally illegal and punishable by heavy penalties but in practice it is recognized as an essential, indeed inevitable, practice to keeping the economy running smoothly. If the intentions of a parallel economy "deal" are to allow production and employment to continue normally and to further the fulfillment of the state plan then the authorities will turn a blind eye.[7]

A second argument used by the believers in repressed inflation is the existence of large and growing savings deposits held by the general public. These suggest that much money cannot be spent and so is saved for security or large scale bulk purchase "deals" when the opportunity arises.[8]

NET INCREASES IN SAVINGS DEPOSITS

1966	1967	1968	1969	1970	1971
4.2	4.0	5.5	6.0	8.2	6.6

Opponents of the repressed inflation thesis argue that the presence of queues is not a symptom of inflation since other goods are in adequate or excess supply. On the contrary, they argue that they are evidence of planning misallocations and distortions which must inevitably occur when consumers are given money rather than ration cards in a centrally planned economy. They say that queues would have to become steadily longer to prove the repressed inflation argument and that black market prices would have to continue to rise.

The final resolution rests on the money supply figures of the Soviet economy, but the Soviet government does not publish these (which is perhaps circumstantial evidence for the repressed inflation thesis). Our own view is that the Soviet Union is constantly in a state of repressed inflation, but the plans are miscoordinated as well; in other words, both sides are right to a point. The first situation, we would suggest, is explicitly used by policymakers as a means of ensuring that all or virtually all of the output of a plan can be sold to consumers regardless of whether it is the kind of product that they really want. And the second is the inevitable result of employing the hybridity of a centrally planned economy (which produces according to a planned scheme) and money, the Western device to lower transaction costs that has the by-product of permitting consumers to indulge their preferences.

There is thus no possibility of this situation changing to any extent in the near future, because the solution to the problem is a general situation of chronic over-supply, which is not likely to occur soon. Recent liberalization of imports from advanced market economies cannot, in our opinion, go very far to resolve the problem, because the Soviets have little that they want to sell to the West and that we wish to buy that could offset the massive balance of payments deficit that would arise from such a policy.

FOOTNOTES

1. In A. S. Shkurko, "The Industrial Wage System in the USSR," *International Labor Review*, November 1964.

2. Samuel Brittan and Peter Lilley, *The Delusion of Incomes Policy* (London: Temple Smith, 1977) p. 106. ". . .In 1950 the average industrial worker over-fulfilled his norm by 39 percent, by 1956 over-fulfillment was 55 percent. The rate of overfulfillments had reached 96 percent in the electro-technical industry, 92 percent in heavy machinery and 82 percent in the automobile industry."

3. P. J. D. Wiles, *Economic Institutions Compared* (Oxford: Basil Blackwell, 1977) p. 372.

4. Michael Jefferson, *Inflation* (London: John Calder, 1977).

5. The anecdotes about queues in communist countries (and other "planned economies") are endless, but here are two examples. "What's fifty yards long and eats potatoes? Answer: Russians in line to buy meat." Or, "A disgruntled Russian, irritated by endless lines to buy food declares that he is fed up and is off to assassinate the local Party Leader. He returns after two hours only to announce that there was a line there too."

6. The best description of the scope and nature of this market we have come across is Dimitri K. Simes, "The Parallel Market," *Survey*, Vol. 21, November 3, 1975.

7. "Samizdat" sources have put the proportion of personal net disposable income spent on the parallel economy at between 10 and 30 percent.

8. From Keith Bush, *Soviet Inflation*, NATO Colloquium on Banking, Money and Credits in Eastern Europe, 1973.

11

Two Democracies in the Second World War

Having already reviewed the many attempts to make price and wage controls work in the two major dictatorships, the Soviet Union and National Socialist Germany (including their wartime efforts), we will examine briefly in this chapter the experience of two of the major democracies, Canada and the United States.

Both Canada and the United States simply followed the lead of all the other wartime powers in setting up various types of economic controls; despite four thousand years of history not one major nation had yet learned the lessons of the past.

CANADA

The Canadian economic controls imposed during the Second World War were among the most wide-ranging efforts at price and wage fixing made by any nation.

"It was a novel experiment, never before attempted in any democratic nation," said one commentator. "Even the German 'price stop' of 1936 had been much less far-reaching . . . ."[1]

The *Maximum Prices Regulations* of December 1, 1941, provided that no good or service could be sold at a price above that charged during the historical period September 15 to October 11, 1941. The price regulations were part of an overall economic mobilization program that included wage and salary controls, income and excess profits taxation, savings campaigns and a massive conservation program encouraging people to "eat it up," "wear it out," "make it do." Setting of production priorities, production directives, raw material allocation, distribution controls and selective service regulations were also part of the overall mobilization effort. In recognition of the fact that the price of imported goods could not be controlled, the government established a system of subsidies to enable it to freeze the domestic price of imported goods. (A similar stance was taken during 1974-1975 by the government of Canada with respect to the price of oil.)

The system of economy-wide controls that the government installed for the purpose of prosecuting the war effort was consciously designed to remove any semblance of market forces from the process of resource allocation. Canada actively encouraged inter-allied economic planning and the communal use of the raw materials available. In short, there was a total commitment to the war and virtually total sacrifice of personal economic freedoms. As K. W. Taylor noted:

> The government, with the overwhelming support of the people, was committed to an all-out war effort . . . .
>
> Reliance on a free price system would have required the government to keep continuously outbidding its citizens. The consequent rapid and accelerating rise in prices would have entailed acute hardship . . . .[2]

There is an element of self-contradiction in these two remarks. Surely, the very best test of the first of these statements would have been the government's reliance on people's free choice in the marketplace rather than on coercion as a means of carrying on the war. The second statement contradicts the first and clearly indicates that, by and large, the population would not have supported the war effort to the extent that it did, without the coercive measures adopted by government. Nevertheless, there was certainly wide-ranging support for the program and people were, it seems, willing to give up their economic freedoms in the short-run for the sake of freedom in the long-run.

As we have seen, mankind has a terrible tendency to forget and hence repeat historical experiences. Human beings also have a tendency to "color" past experiences—the "good old days" phenomenon being a good example of this sort of behavior. In looking back on the war years there seems to be an assumption that wage and price controls "worked"—that they accomplished something that would not have occurred in their absence. It is certainly true that production controls "worked" in the sense that large volumes of resources were devoted to the production of war *materiel*. It is not clear, however, that this redirection of resources was accomplished without the inflation that would have occurred had there been no controls.

An interesting test of the idea that controls reduced the inflation associated with the Second World War is provided by a comparison of that inflation with the inflation during the period of the First World War. The impression given by the cost of living indices is that, overall, the control program adopted during the Second World War had the effect of preventing the surge in prices that was associated with the First World War. Notably, the controls did not keep prices from ultimately rising by about the same amount. There is reason to believe, however, that there was much more inflation during the Second World War than is suggested by the price index. In the words of one scholar:

> No matter how rigidly prices were held in check, costs tended to creep up . . . . The major attack on this problem was along the lines of simplification and standardization in both production and distribution . . . reducing the number of varieties or models, cutting out frills, minimizing the use of scarce materials . . . every class of industry was affected.[3]

In other words there was a conscious effort to reduce the quality of every commodity that Canadians bought, to prevent the quoted prices from "creeping up." Since it is clear that quality degradation was used to cut costs, what are we to make of the "reported" price index? K. W. Taylor has explained that:

> It would be impossible to give any quantitative expression to the savings in man-power, materials or money which these orders achieved, but they were very considerable and undoubtedly were of major importance in enabling the Board . . . to "hold the line" effectively.[4]

Accordingly, all that we can say for sure is that the official statistics for the rate of inflation during the Second World War represent a "considerable" under-estimate of the true inflation situation. Therefore, the straight-forward comparison of the official statistics is not a totally meaningful exercise. In spite of this, the statistics indicate that after the "smoke had cleared," prices had risen by about the same amount over both war periods. We must, therefore, seriously question whether the controls did indeed have much effect. In any event, it cannot simply be accepted that, even under those stringent wartime conditions, controls were successsful.

THE UNITED STATES

From the time the United States began preparing for World War II, the Roosevelt Administration delayed imposing price and wage controls for almost two years. This reluctance may well have been stimulated by the example of Germany and Italy; restrictions on personal freedom were not altogether welcome in the midst of an all-out war in defense of freedom. From January 1941 until October 1942, the government attempted to restrain the inevitable rises in both prices and wages by "voluntary" controls and moral persuasion.

During that period wholesale prices rose almost 24 percent and consumer prices more than 18 percent. With the establishment of the Office of Price Administration and the imposition of strict controls, however, consumer prices rose 8.7 percent between October 1942 and August 1945.

Wartime price controls proved *relatively* effective (*at least on the surface*), principally due to the immense patriotism which shored them up. The rationing system was an important element since it curtailed demand and introduced "point-money" as a factor. Without rationing prices would have risen much higher. Even so, hourly wage rates in manufacturing rose 14.7 percent in that 35 month period until August 1945.[5] The rise in prices was not as steep because some manufacturers lowered the quality of goods while not raising the official selling price, and many persons engaged in the black market, paying very high prices to get what they wanted when they wanted it. Such ways of circumventing the official rules have obviously been practiced over the last forty centuries and, when we consider price controls in the modern economy, it will be apparent that quality change makes it much more likely for the *nominal* (*if not the real*) prices of commodities to appear to be held down (and hence, for the policy of controls to be perceived as a success).

Milton Friedman, in discussing the results of wartime controls, stressed this phenomenon when he pointed out that, in reality, individual price and wage changes cannot be prevented.

> In the main, price changes will simply be concealed by taking the form of changes in discounts, service, and quality, and wage changes, in overtime, perquisites and so on. Even 60,000 bureaucrats backed by 300,000 volunteers plus widespread patriotism were unable during World War Two to cope with the ingenuity of millions of people in finding ways to get around price and wage controls that conflicted with their individual sense of justice.[6]

But as controls are relaxed and the demand for traditional quality reasserts itself, prices inevitably rise once more.

After the war was over, the pent-up inflation burst and the controls broke down completely. From August 1945 to November 1946, wholesale prices rose more than 32 percent and consumer prices almost 18.6 percent.[7] It is entirely possible that the end result would have been almost the same by the year 1946 if controls had never been introduced in the first place. There would have been the advantage also, that this "open inflation," as Professor Hayek calls it, makes economic dealings and resource allocation much easier and more susceptible to conscious, rational methods. The trouble with "repressed inflation" which one finds under the regime of price and wage controls is that it is impossible to predict what pent-up inflation will spring itself upon the economy when the controls are removed.

FOOTNOTES

1. K. W. Taylor, "Canadian War-time Price Controls, 1941–46," *Canadian Journal of Economics and Political Science*, February 1947, p. 87.

2. *Ibid.*, p. 85.

3. *Ibid.*, p. 91.

4. *Ibid.*, p. 92.

5. U.S. Department of Labor, Bureau of Labor Statistics, *Handbook of Labor Statistics* (Washington, D.C., 1947); *Ibid.*, *Bulletin* 916 (Washington, D.C., 1948) pp. 107–8 and 54; *Monthly Labor Review*, November 1943, p. 879; November 1945, p. 1045; November 1947, p. 609.

6. Milton Friedman, *An Economist's Protest*, p. 126.

7. U.S. Department of Labor, *op. cit.*

12

Postwar Rent Controls

The rent which a landlord charges for his accommodation is merely an instance of a price for a commodity, like all other prices for all other commodities. And like all other prices and all other commodities, rents have been a prime target for government restrictions. The postwar experience with rent control has been particularly revealing in regard to the adequacy of controls in general.

Governments have three main reasons for imposing rent control. The first is the fear that those who can pay will get all the housing and the poor will be left in the cold. The second is that landlords benefit too much from rents which can be indefinitely raised. The third is that a rise in rents is a form of inflation, and so should not be allowed.

THE HOUSING RECORD OF SAN FRANCISCO

In a particularly penetrating article[1] Milton Friedman and George Stigler examined the housing record of San Francisco. After the earthquake of April 18, 1906, the heart of the city was utterly destroyed by fire. Some 225,000 people were homeless. "Yet," say the authors, "when one turns to the *San Francisco Chronicle* of May 24, 1906—the first available issue after the earthquake—there is not a single mention of a housing shortage! The classified advertisments listed 64 offers (some for more than one dwelling) of flats and houses for rent, and 19 of houses for sale, against five advertisements of flats or houses wanted. Then and thereafter a considerable number of all types of accommodation except hotel rooms were offered for rents."

In 1906, San Francisco allowed the free market mechanism to allocate accommodation, allowing rents to find their own level after the disaster. Even so, there was a great deal of low-cost accommodation available in San Francisco at that time. (Friedman and Stigler quote the 1906 advertisement "Six-room house and bath, with 2 additional rooms in basement having fire-places, nicely furnished; fine piano;. . .$45.")

To take another example of housing shortage, in 1946 the population of San Francisco had increased by about a third in six years as people migrated westward. The problem was much less severe than the 1906 shortage, at least on paper. But the newspapers billed the shortage as "the most critical problem facing California." Advertisements for apartments to rent ran at about one-sixteenth of the 1906 level, while advertisements of houses for sale were up threefold. In 1906 after the earthquake, there was one "wanted for rent" for every ten "houses or apartments for rent"; in 1946, there were 375 "wanted for rent" for every ten "for rent."

Why the disparity? Because in 1906, rents in San Francisco were free to rise. In 1946, the use of higher rents to ration housing had been made illegal by the imposition of rent ceilings.

And what of the arguments against the allocation of housing by price? The first is very questionable: as Friedman and Stigler observe, "At all times during the acute shortage in 1906, inexpensive flats and houses were available." The second is misleading. Of course landlords do benefit from a shortage like that of 1906. But the ultimate solution of a housing shortage must be the construction of new property, and nobody will construct new houses for rent if he is denied, through rent control, an attractive return on his money. As for the third argument, that high rents are a form of inflation, it must be observed that one does not keep prices down in an economy merely by taking commodities off the market, as rent controls do.

SCANDINAVIAN HOUSES

Rent control was introduced in Sweden in 1942 as an "emergency" and temporary regulation. At least until the end of the Socialist government in 1976, it was still in effect. The wartime housing shortage reached its peak in 1942 and seems to have become much worse over the period that controls had been operating.

In Sweden, the record of rent control speaks for itself. Says Sven Rydenfelt:[2]

> To the economist, it seems self-evident that a price control like the Swedish rent control must lead to a demand surplus, that is, a housing shortage. For a long period the general public was more inclined to believe that the shortage was a result of the abnormal situation created by the war, and this even in a non-participating country like Sweden. . . . This opinion does not, however, accord with the evidence. . . that the shortage during the war years was insignificant compared with that after the war. It was only in the post-war years that the housing shortage assumed such proportions that it became Sweden's most serious social problem.

The main demand-effect of Swedish rent controls has been to draw a huge number of single people—who would be more inclined to live with their families were rents allowed to rise—into the housing market.

Professor Frank Knight commented[3] on the phenomenon: "If educated people can't or won't see that fixing a price below the market level inevitably creates a 'shortage' . . . it is hard to believe in the usefulness of telling them anything whatever in this field of discourse."

86

RENT CONTROLS IN BRITAIN

Rent controls were first introduced to Britain in December 1915, prohibiting landlords to charge rents higher than those charged in August 1914, when the Great War broke out on the Continent of Europe. After the war, controls were relaxed to some extent, but new controls were imposed on September 1, 1939.

The economic effects of rent controls were (as Professor Paish notes)[4] inadequate maintenance, reduction in mobility, and fewer houses to let.

In recent years the situation has become more and more complicated. In the first place, public housing has become so heavily relied upon as a means of meeting the inevitable shortage which followed controls that some 42 percent of the population of the United Kingdom now live in publicly-owned housing; in Scotland, the proportion is 48 percent. Minimal rents are charged to these tenants. Private landlords are thus forced to compete with an ultra-low-cost housing alternative, which explains why the waiting lists for public housing are so long (a normal wait is several years) and why landlords are withdrawing their property from the market.

Another series of restrictions derives from the government's attempts to tidy up the undesirable effects of restrictions themselves. When landlords cannot extract an adequate profit margin from their properties, then they let the buildings deteriorate, attempt to squeeze more tenants into the same building, and try to find ways around the rent restrictions. Hence the phenomenon of "Rachmanism" which hit Britain in the early sixties. To deal with these effects, it was thought necessary to introduce a new Rent Act in 1965, which gave security of tenure to many tenants. At the same time, rents of property not covered by the earlier regulations were "regulated"—that is, a "fair rent" was fixed and could be appealed from time to time by the landlord or the tenant. Since 1972, nearly all unfurnished rented property has been put under this rent regulation mechanism. And what has happened? The Francis Committee on the Rent Acts[5] published a table showing that the number of unfurnished vacancies advertised in the *London Weekly Advertiser* fell from 767 to 66 in the seven years up to 1970. In the same period, the number of furnished vacancies has increased from 855 to 1,290. "It is strange," is the cynical comment of F. G. Pennance,[6] "that the Francis Committee forebore to draw the obvious conclusion—that rent regulation *had* affected supply." And it had affected it for the worse. British landlords have become very reluctant to put their property up for rent, because the security of tenure offered to their customers means that they will often have difficulty in reclaiming the house. Nobody could estimate the numbers of landlords - especially small-scale operators - who have been driven from the housing market.

OTHER EFFECTS OF RENT CONTROL

Many other severe side-effects of rent control are easily seen, other than mere shortage of housing.

The first is that controls, originally designed to help the poorer tenants, have now precipitated a situation in which many landlords are in fact poorer than their own tenants. For example, Dr. Willys Knight found in his study of Lansing, Michigan, that the median income of tenants was greater than the median income of landlords.[7] While the difference might be due to the effect of age (landlords are older and hence many of them have no income except rent), the encouragement of this difference does not seem to be a sensible way to solve our housing shortages. B. Bruce-Briggs, an urbanologist with the Hudson Institute, asserts flatly that "From the first, rent control [in New York] was actually a subsidy to the working and middle classes. . .partially levied on the very poor."[8]

The second is that artificially low rents lead to misallocation of housing resources. Persons do not need to move into smaller apartments to reduce their rents, because rents are low. Similarly, homeowners with one or two spare rooms which they would rent out to single persons will not enter the housing market because they do not receive a sufficient return to justify the expense of repairs and redecoration. These and other effects generate a situation in which many individuals and families are homeless, while perfectly good accommodation is withdrawn from the market.

With the lack of money in the housing market comes lack of adequate facilities. In his 1942 essay on French rent controls, de Jouvenal[9] observed that controls meant that middle-class apartments with three or four reception rooms frequently cost about $2 a month. "Rent seldom rises above 4 per cent of any income," he commented. "Frequently it is less than 1 per cent." In Paris at that time there were about 16,000 buildings in such disrepair that they could only be demolished. And 82 percent of Parisians had no bath or shower; more than half had outside lavatories, and a fifth had no running water. The owners, who were not in a financial position to keep up their own buildings, could hardly be blamed.

As the capital stock deteriorates, slums are born. Since no economic incentive exists for owners to repair run-down properties in declining areas, the blight spreads. As the blight spreads, more and more buildings become uninhabitable. The effect of rent controls is ultimately to remove once-habitable dwellings from the housing stock.

THE DECLINE OF NEW YORK

These effects can be seen to have contributed to the demise of one city in particular, namely New York. Federal rent control went into effect there in November 1943 and the state took over its administration in May 1950. In 1962, the city became the administrator: in so doing, it made a stick to beat itself. The damage done by controls "cannot be properly assessed in dollars-and-cents alone. As even the hapless officials responsible now reluctantly concede, rent control is costing the City of New York, through abandonment and ultimate destruction, upwards of 30,000 dwelling units *annually*."[10]

Social effects in New York are both severe—as the crumbling tenements make clear—and subtle: by setting tenant against landlord, rent control fans the flames of social hatred and class warfare in a city once known as the nation's melting pot.

Urbanologist B. Bruce-Briggs has concisely summed up the consequences of rent control in New York City. He notes that:

> Rent control reduces mobility by encouraging tenants to stay put. It also encourages people to occupy more space than they otherwise would. It offers the landlord incentives not to provide adequate services; he must be forced to do so by law, leading to endless litigation. (In 1975 nearly a half-million cases went to New York's Housing Court.) Rent control must be administered, at a cost of $13 million to New York City and State. It creates unimaginable costs for tenants and landlords in time and administrative fees. It has resulted in massive tax delinquency.[11]

Economic effects on the city itself are far-reaching. "Maximum Base Rents" are rarely increased by more than 8.5 percent per annum. In contrast, according to *Barron's*[12], "taxes and labor are rising at well over 10 percent per year, while in the past 18 months, the price of fuel oil, a ponderable part of total operating costs, has soared by 2000 percent. Small wonder that more and more buildings are being run at a loss, while tax delinquency, once largely confined to one or two rotten boroughs, has spread far and wide." Real estate tax delinquencies for fiscal year 1974–75 were estimated at $220 million, up from $148 million and $122 million in the two preceding years.

When government agencies insist that their policies have kept down the cost of accommodation, it seems fair to ask that costs such as these be taken into consideration. Rent controls in the postwar period, like most price and wage restrictions, have turned out to be an expensive failure.

FOOTNOTES

1. M. Friedman and G. Stigler, "Roofs or Ceilings? The Current Housing Problem," *Popular Essays on Current Problems*, Vol. 1, No. 2 (Irvington-on-Hudson: Foundation for Economic Education, 1946).

2. Sven Rydenfelt, "Rent Controls Thirty Years On," *Verdict on Rent Control* (London: Institute of Economic Affairs, 1972). See also a Canadian version of this valuable work entitled *Rent Control–A Popular Paradox* (Vancouver, British Columbia: The Fraser Institute, 1975).

3. Frank H. Knight, "Truth and Relevance at Bay," *American Economic Review*, December 1949, p. 274.

4. F. W. Paish, "The Economics of Rent Restriction," *Lloyds Bank Review*, April 1950.

5. *Report of the Committee on the Rent Acts*, Cmnd. 4609, H.M.S.O. London, 1971, p. 8.

6. Introduction to *Verdict on Rent Control*, *op. cit.*

7. W. Knight, *Postwar Rent Control Controversy*, Research Paper 23 (Atlanta: Georgia State College School of Business, 1962).

8. B. Bruce-Briggs, "Rent Control Must Go," *The New York Times Magazine*, April 18, 1976. There are of course many anecdotal "horror stories" to illustrate this all too common phenomenon (the sad fact that many social programs designed to help the poor do the exact opposite in practice). The author offers his own pet example:

> My favorite freeloader is a good friend who earns more than $30,000 a year. He has possession of a rent-controlled apartment in Yorkville which he rarely uses, since he prefers to live in his mistress's penthouse in the East 50's. He would be a fool to give up the rent-controlled apartment—they may split—so he uses it as an occasional office or *pied-à-terre*, lends it to friends, or occasionally subleases it for a short period of time. When asked to justify this, he will look you straight in the eye and tell you about the needs of the old people in rent-controlled apartments on his block.

9. Bertrand de Jouvenal, "No Vacancies" (Irvington-on-Hudson: Foundation for Economic Education, 1962).

10. *Barron's*, October 27, 1975, p. 7.

11. B. Bruce-Briggs, *op. cit.*

12. *Barron's*, *op. cit.*

13

A Postwar Survey of Six Continents

GREAT BRITAIN: 1945–1968

Up to 1964, British incomes policy was aimed primarily at curbing inflation by checking the rise in wages. Soon after Atlee's government took office after the Second World War, this process began. In 1948 the government issued qualitative guidelines stating the conditions which wage increases would have to satisfy in order to be declared in line with the public interest. The Trades Union Congress, working with its political wing, accepted these guidelines "with remarkable fidelity."[1]

Nevertheless, this voluntary wage freeze led to disgruntlement in the unions over the course of time, since the cost of living was still rising despite the wage agreement. Restraint collapsed on many occasions, and in its September 1950 conference, the TUC formally quitted all agreements. The success of the first British experiment with wage guidelines was short-lived indeed.

In 1952, the chairman of Lloyds Bank in London put the results of controls over the British economy in a clear perspective:

> There cannot really be any dispute about the superior *efficiency* of a properly working price system. . . . Rationing and controls are merely methods of *organizing* scarcity; the price system automatically works toward *overcoming* scarcity. If a commodity is in short supply, a rise in its price does not merely reduce demand but will also stimulate an increase in its supply. In this, the price system stands in direct contrast with rationing and controls, which tend to make it less profitable or less attractive in other ways, to engage in essential production than to produce the inessentials which are left uncontrolled.[2]

There was a long break without any controls (except for a short intervention by the new Council on Prices, Productivity and Incomes in 1957) until 1961, when a new balance of payments crisis urged the then Conservative party government to bring back wage restraint. The famous Macmillan "pay pause" was ordered for civil servants. The measure did not, however, achieve its expectations; it did not improve the morale of the private sector and irritated public employees. The

91

Trades Union Congress, which the government hoped would follow the lead, said, "No deal."

"Incomes Policy: The Next Step" was the title of a 1962 government White Paper which explained the next venture in incomes policy in the U.K. This was to limit annual wage increases to a maximum of about two percent.

The maximum was, however, a matter of academic interest only. The hourly average wage rate rose by about four and a half percent.

By way of compromise, the National Economic Development Council set a target of four percent growth for the British economy, and declared that wage increases of three or three and a half percent would not be inconsistent with the target. But this, too, was unsuccessful. The rate of growth was much less, and in 1964, average hourly earnings rose by over eight percent.[3]

The fact that wages so outstripped productivity might be one reason for the continued poor performance of that economy even today. As the London *Economist* underlined:

> In the first five months of this year [1966] more people in Britain pushed up their earnings more steeply for less work than at any time since 1960. . . . This is what has happened to the incomes policy. . . . The plain fact is that since Labour took office in October 1964, hourly earnings have risen 2¼ times faster than that of output. . . .[4]

Something had to be done. And in 1966, the government ordered a complete freeze in wages and prices, salaries and dividends, to be followed by a period of "severe restraint" of six months or more. In the short term, the government achieved its objective, and the index of hourly earnings remained fairly stable at 169.8 (January 1965 = 100). "But," as Eric Schiff complains, "in the following six months of 'severe restraint,' the pent-up pressure could no longer be fully restrained. The indexes of hourly earnings rose to 173.1 in May, for an increase of about 1.9 percent. . . ."[5] And over the next two years the pressure continued, such that "Over the full year ending April 1968, according to the Annual Report of the National Board for Prices and Incomes[6], hourly earnings had risen over 8 percent—hardly what had been expected after a year during which the general official rate for wage increases was zero."[7]

FRANCE AFTER 1960

Eric Schiff summarizes the French experience with wage targets as follows:

> The fifth regular Plan of Economic and Social Development, due to appear around 1960, could not be worked out according to schedule. Instead, an Interim Plan was set up, which. . . envisaged, for the immediate future, an annual increase of 4 percent in the average wage level. Had actual average wage increases in the years immediately following 1960 been approximately in line with this guidepost, rising unit labor costs as a cause of inflation would,

in fact, have been removed. The rise in labor productivity actually achieved during those years would have sufficed to produce this result. But the actual annual average wage increases were too far above the guideline rate. In the five year period 1959 to 1963 they were, in this order, 6.2%, 7.1%, 7.9%, 9.5%, 7.9%. The updrift in prices continued.[8]

And in the Fifth Plan itself, new targets were agreed upon; an average rise of 1.5 percent in the general price level was set as the acceptable maximum. The average annual rise in the GNP deflator would be kept below 2.7 percent.

The Sixth Plan decrees that a 1.7 percent increase in industrial prices would be acceptable, equivalent to about a 2.5 percent increase in prices. There is, however, no mention of wage guidelines within the text of the Plan.

Prices in France have continued to rise in the 1970s: the consumer price index registered a 5.4 percent increase in 1971, and from thence the average increases have been edging up—6.0 percent, 7.4 percent, 13.6 percent, 11.8 percent. French authorities responded by implementing a three-month freeze on prices and wages, coupled with a 6.5 percent ceiling on wage and price increases in 1977. *Le Monde* commented that "the Barre [France's Prime Minister] plan rather resembles the measures Giscard D'Estaing took in December 1972 and December 1973 when he was Finance Minister. . . ."[9]

The editor of *Barron's*, Mr. Robert M. Bleiberg, (in his issue for April 18, 1977, p. 7) summed up the recent French experience very well when he wrote:

> First comes the inevitable official denial. In mid-September, [1976] Dr. Raymond Barre, Finance Minister and Premier, gave a reassuring speech in which he promised that his anti-inflationary program would hinge on traditional fiscal and monetary restraints. Just four weeks later he unveiled a price freeze, which, in theory at any rate, lasted until the end of the year.
>
> Like so many of its predecessors, the Barre program, regardless of what the unions profess to believe, is heavily weighted against capital and for labor. Thus, while prices are controlled by statute, wages are subject only to secondary, informal restraints. Finally, the program has led to painfully familiar results. After a few months of relative stability, largely reflecting a cut in the value-added tax, the price indices once again have begun to climb. According to a recent bulletin by S. J. Rundt & Associates, knowledgeable observers of foreign exchange and international trade: "After relatively moderate increases of 0.3% in both December and January, the retail price index in February shot up by 0.7%, and there is every indication that its climb in March and April will also turn out to be on the hefty side, partly because there have been substantial increases in wholesale prices which have yet to work their way through to the retail price level, and partly because the costs of a number of public services are scheduled to go up by 6½% in April." To nobody's surprise

(except, perhaps, that of the powers-that-be), the French franc has been weak.

Prime Minister Barre has since embarked on a number of economic reforms which, if carried through, will considerably liberalize the French economy and earn for him a reputation as the French Ludwig Erhard. He has had the audacity to remove controls on bread, the price of which had been fixed by the French state since 1791. It will be interesting to watch the end result of the new French reform program.

CONTROLS ELSEWHERE IN EUROPE

"Austria's economy at the end of World War II was characterized by low levels of production, excess money supply, and high rates of inflation."[10] In July 1945, price control was transferred to the Austrian government, and the law was immediately applied to foodstuffs, raw materials and services. The cost of living indices of officially controlled prices and the indices of net hourly earnings rose 14 percent between April 1945 and April 1946.[11]

In January 1946, wage control was assumed by the Austrian government, and the first wage and price agreement was concluded in 1947. New prices were established for food, rent, coal and public utilities. In each of the successive years until 1951, additional agreements were concluded. The consumer price index continued to rise. In 1949, it rose 22.1 percent. In 1950, it rose 14.6 percent. In 1951, it rose 27.6 percent. In 1952, it rose 13 percent.

In 1962 the government of Denmark adopted an incomes policy on a comprehensive scale. In the decade preceding the controls, the rate of inflation in Denmark had averaged about 2.5 percent per annum, although it had suffered wide fluctuations. But between 1958 and 1965, that country had the sharpest average annual rate of increase in unit labor costs of a group of thirteen Western countries examined by the U.N. Economic Commission for Europe.[12] In the sixties, the cost of living index subsided once more, but large balance of payments deficits troubled the Danish government.

In 1963 the Danish Parliament took a series of wage and price measures to chill wage agreements (but not quite to freeze them) and that year was all quiet on the wage front. But in 1964 the wage and price spiral started to twist again; consumer prices rose by steadily increasing amounts: in 1964, by 3.1 percent, in 1965 by 5.4 percent, then 7 percent, then 8.2, then 8.0, with relaxation only in the early seventies.

The Dutch experience with wage controls has been painful. Up to 1959, the government laid down guidelines for wage agreements after examining the overall prospects for the economy. In that year, the system was changed by linking permitted wage increases to productivity levels in the particular sector.

Unfortunately this system proved too difficult to administer—for one thing, government and workers could never agree on the genuine productivity figures—and in 1963 the system was supplanted. The new approach was much like the old: a Central Planning Bureau and the Social and Economic Council examined the possibilities for wage increases, and their approved ceilings were mandatory, with transgressors being prosecuted. All that these limits tended to do, however, was to drive employers and employees to deal in undeclared wage transfers and to deter secondary workers from joining the labor force. A shortage of labor left the market very tight indeed. As Schiff again says:

> Open "wage explosion" was not slow in coming. In the autumn of 1963 the government set a guideline of 6 percent for the average wage increase in the following year. But a number of employers, in open defiance of the guideline, offered higher wages. Attempts by the Board of Government Mediators to use its legal power to intervene were of no avail. The final overall result of the protracted wage bargaining of 1964 was an average wage increase of about 15 percent. . . .[13]

THE UNITED STATES: 1950–1969

Much the same picture could be seen when the United States imposed price and wage controls during the Korean hostilities. In June 1950, when the war began, the Consumer Price Index stood at 177.8. Half a year later, when controls went into effect, the Index was at the level of 184.7. In September of 1952 when the pay freeze ended, the Consumer Price Index had reached 191.1. Apparently, that set of controls had no effect on the rate of inflation.

At that time, the Truman Administration believed that wage increases, in order not to be inflationary, must not exceed the trend of economy-wide productivity gains. One OECD survey of the period says:

> The Kennedy Administration. . . elaborated the more explicit formulation that the general guide for non-inflationary wage behavior is that the increase in wage rates (including fringe benefits) in each industry is equal to the trend rate of overall productivity increase. The general guide for non-inflationary price behavior calls for price reductions if the industry's rate of productivity increase exceeds the overall rate. . . it calls for an appropriate increase in prices if the opposite relationship prevails; and it calls for stable prices if the two rates of productivity increase are equal.[14]

These "guide-posts" were originally conceived to be purely for information's sake, but eventually the government found itself giving out more and more information about rates of economic growth and productivity variation, and then it found itself increasingly involved in specific bargaining and pricing situations.

Prices rose once more in the mid-sixties, and confrontations between the government and the labor unions became more and more frequent. The guideline effort, at least in the form initiated in 1962, was given up for dead when in 1966 the airline mechanics refused a wage offer which was far in excess of the guidelines, but which was nevertheless approved by the government of the day.

Thereafter, no definite guidelines were published and only rough suggestions were offered on an *ad hoc* basis to particular organizations.

The guideline policy was at best unhelpful and according to economist Arthur Okun, positively harmful. He says that the governmental attempts to influence private bargaining and pricing decisions accounted for a substantial portion of the acceleration in prices between 1968 and 1969, as the repressed inflation worked itself out.[15]

CONTROLS IN ARGENTINA

On the South American continent, similar controls were tried and failed. Perhaps the most celebrated inflation rate in that part of the world belongs to Argentina, despite the price-fixing attempts of the administration of Juan Peron. But his controls, which lasted (on and off) from 1946 to 1955, did not mollify it. As Congressman Philip Crane said in the House of Representatives on the subject of the United States' Economic Stabilization measures:

> In June 1947, the [Argentine] government instituted a program of fixing retail prices and seized factory stocks of clothing and shoes for distribution at these prices. Numerous price violators were arrested. Then, in an attempt to control prices, the Government began to subsidize foodstuffs in the 1948-49 period. It bought wheat from the farmers and sold it to the miller in an attempt to control the price of bread. The same policy was followed with regard to meat, cooking oils, and the milk supply. The controls did not work and in 1949 all public services, including railroads, increased prices. The cost of other commodities increased: Gasoline rose from 35 to 60 centavos per liter, bread from 50 to 80 centavos per loaf, meat from 1.80 pesos to 2.50 pesos, and clothing prices soared.[16]

At the end of the 1940s, Peron supported increases in wages although he tried to keep them down as far as possible. An example of the ineffectiveness of this policy was his grant of a sixty percent wage increase to workers in the important sugar industry. The military also received substantial increases, and this sparked off a new round of pay demands.

Despite his control of the General Confederation of Labor, Peron could not continue to hold down wages; his demand in 1954 that wage increases should be tied to a very low target precipitated an epidemic of wildcat strikes in many industries. And because of his failures, Peron lost support in the country, and resigned under military pressure on September 19, 1955.

ISRAEL: THREE DECADES OF CONTROLS

Israel has experienced almost uninterrupted, serious inflation ever since its birth in 1948; yet despite this, it has had a history of extensive wage and price controls.[17]

The first measures were enacted in April 1949 when the government announced that the new republic would set maximum prices for most goods and have rationing for "essentials," such as, clothing, food, and raw materials. Whereas these controls were originally accepted with relief by the population, the underlying, continued growth in the money supply meant that constant inflationary pressure led to increases in costs and squeezed the profit margins of producers. Gradually a black market began to form in a sizable number of price-regulated goods.

During 1949 and 1950 the official prices of some essentials were actually reduced in absolute terms, thus exacerbating the shortages and forcing more goods onto the black market. As more people found that they had to trade on the black market, their real cost of living became less and less reflected in the official cost of living index. By enlarging the relative size of the black market, the price reductions (as always, well-intended) actually increased rather than reduced the cost of living. [18]

The price controls also induced large influxes of imports as the rationing system for domestic goods led to more and more people buying foreign substitutes. Then, to make matters worse, the domestic supply of agricultural produce was badly hit by a drought in 1951. [19]

Eventually the government was forced to reassess its policy and in 1951 prices were allowed to move upward and monetary policy was tightened.

In operation, the price controls had revealed all the familiar signs of a slip into arbitrary state power. A large bureaucracy (3,000 officials for a population of 1.4 million) was recruited to administer the controls; the public was encouraged to turn in violators; to catch evaders, road blocks were set up, mass arrests were made, and special courts were established to try them. [20]

The controls also diminished the efficiency of the economy by precipitating the cartelization of some sectors of industry and encouraging people to engage in such activities as barter, in-kind transactions, quality reductions and the other standard types of evasion.

Between 1951 and 1953 the relaxation of controls led to a rise of 150 percent in the cost of living official index. But this overstated the real increase for the vast majority of the public, because they had previously been trading on the black market and paying far higher prices than the official cost index indicated. [21]

Thus, price controls at first made the official cost of living index *understate* the real cost of living and then made it *overstate* it. Nevertheless, by 1953 the annual inflation rate was down to 28 percent, according to official figures.

The subsequent period (1956–1961) was an era of steady growth and falling unemployment. By 1959 price control had been completely abolished although fiscal measures had come into use to manipulate some prices and, to an extent, this was a disguised form of price control.

Further inflationary monetary policy in the period after 1960 led to an ineffective devaluation in 1962 and a call for voluntary wage restraint. In 1963 wages and prices were officially frozen although average wages rose 10.5 percent; in 1964 wages were subjected to a 5 percent guideline (but still rose 11 percent). The squeeze on profits that this imposed led to a recession during 1966.[22]

From 1967 to 1969 there was a rigorously applied wage freeze. The government capitalized fully on patriotic emotion arising from the six-day war and this particular period in Israeli history appears to have been the only one for which proponents could claim any success for wage-price controls. However, it must be noted that the national unity induced by the war and the presence of high unemployment and fiscal restraint were special factors which doubtless helped considerably.[23]

After 1969 inflation rose again and culminated in 1971 with the devaluation of the currency and the reinstitution of wage and price controls. Despite the government's announced intention to limit price increases to a 4-8 percent annual range, inflation continued rising and excess money was diverted, as it had been from 1963–65, into the property markets. At one point, construction firms were sometimes selling new apartments two to three years in advance, but upon the advent of controls they held back. The selling prices of second-hand apartments, which were unregulated, thereby skyrocketed.[24]

By 1972 the failure of these controls was clear and they were removed.

In the mid-1970s Israeli inflation has been particularly severe, rising to nearly 40 percent in 1974. Since then the world slump has had the effect of mollifying Israeli inflation to a great extent. In summary, the experience of Israel can be seen to be another case of the failure of wage and price controls. Israeli history has been marked by a rate of inflation considerably higher than the international average for industrial countries, which in turn has been the result of lax monetary policy and considerable distortion in the economy during the time that controls were in force. The extent of the distortion and of the misallocation of resources has been directly related to the severity and duration of controls.[25]

AUSTRALIA: A FREEZE THAT FAILED

From 1921 to 1953 Australia had an "incomes policy" of a sort. The Australian basic wage was adjusted automatically, every quarter, as the consumer price index changed. In April 1975, the indexing of wages was renewed and still continues although it is a system which has been controversial in recent years.

From the end of the Second World War to 1973 there was no active policy of government price controls. The Prices Justification Tribunal was established in 1973; this was the first attempt at price controls (this time on a voluntary basis) in almost three decades.

On April 13, 1977, the Australian government imposed a "freeze" on prices and wages which lasted just 41 days. It was widely denounced as one of the most dismal attempts to control prices in the long and unhappy tradition of wage and price controls. An Australian economist, Peter Samuel, concisely summed up this short and foolish episode of Australian economic history.

The proximate causes of the "thaw" of the "freeze" lie in its inherent absurdity. No one had thought how to freeze prices determined flexibly by auction and tender every day—such as the prices of a whole range of food products, building jobs and contracted services. What to do about imports whose prices are beyond anyone's powers to "freeze"? And what about price rises "in the pipeline", approved by government regulatory bodies, or notified, but not yet in effect?

Some large shopping chains, foolishly seeking popular acclaim and publicity boldly announced they would pay no more for any of their stocks, whereupon it not surprisingly transpired that they quickly started to run short of many lines. There was enormous confusion about the details of how the freeze was supposed to work.

It was originally said that the freeze was to be dependent on everyone agreeing to stop raising prices and wages; that business would not be expected to freeze their prices if the costs of inputs were not also frozen. It was also declared to be voluntary. Both principles were quickly abandoned. One business which declared that it could not abide by the freeze on prices, was viciously denounced and threatened with retaliatory action. The unions denounced the scheme and it was quickly clear that the whole thing was a chaotic gimmick, lots of noise and little thought or action. Its end was acknowledged on May 24th, just 41 days after its inauguration. The Arbitration Commission and the unions put the final torpedoes into an already sinking hulk and few mourned its disappearance.

The major lesson to be learned is that many of our leaders and opinion-makers live in a mental world of medieval delusions. They sometimes denounce the market economy as "nineteenth century economics", but their thinking is far more primitive. In imposing such madness as the "freeze" they reveal themselves captive to primitivist notions of the existence of objectively "just" prices and wages and guild-type concepts of regulation. Historians of economic thought would probably date their thinking as somewhere in the fourteenth century.[26]

EGYPT: THE WHEEL OF HISTORY TURNS FULL CIRCLE

Forty and fifty centuries ago, Egypt's rulers instituted a plethora of government controls over economic activity; the pharaohs attempted to keep down the price of food in times of shortages, with but limited success.

The successors of Ramses II who rule from the modern capital of Cairo are facing the same economic problems that have plagued governments since the beginning of recorded history.

Egypt in 1977 had a GNP of $11 billion a year but was struggling to subsidize its citizens to the extent of $1.2 billion in cash (which went to lower the prices of food and other necessities); in addition the state-owned industries lost over

$1.37 billion the previous year.[27]

Price controls have resulted in extreme shortages of fruits and vegetables in the cities. Farmers refuse to bring goods to market if they can't receive a fair price for their labor and investment, as they have refused from time immemorial. The artificially low price of bread has resulted in people in the cities going hungry and has had some unforeseen side effects.

According to *The Washington Post*:

> A staple of the Egyptian diet is a rough loaf of bread made with coarse flour that sells for a few pennies because it is heavily subsidized by the government. Its weight and price are fixed by law.
>
> Some bakers are cheating by shorting the weight without cutting prices and using the extra flour to make higher-profit items like pastries. In rural villages, according to newspaper reports, peasants who in the past baked their own bread are buying in markets because the subsidy makes it cheaper. But the real problem is that the subsidized bread is so cheap that cattle breeders are using it for fodder.
>
> It's about a third the price of hay, which is so expensive it has been driving up the price of meat, and since the bread can be purchased in unrestricted amounts, it's going to the animals instead of to the people.
>
> In a wry commentary on this situation, a newspaper cartoon depicted a group of barnyard cows eating round loaves of bread, with one of them observing, "This people food isn't any good unless it's washed down with 7-Up."
>
> The government cannot cut the bread subsidy because that would drive the price up beyond the reach of many families, especially urban workers, who depend on it. But it is looking for ways to control abuses.
>
> The Ministry of Supply authorized an increase in the flour allocations to all provinces, and ordered surveillance teams to inspect the bakeries and make sure they produce authorized products at full capacity.

Egyptian bureaucrats began to wonder if something was wrong in 1975, we are told.

> "We started to review the thing," an informed official of the Ministry of Economy said, "when we realized that the fancy cake sold at the Hilton Hotel to rich tourists was made with subsidized flour, subsidized sugar and subsidized shortening."[29]

The government is now looking into various ways to solve a number of problems which have arisen because of their price and wage control system. An official has been quoted as saying that ". . . the system's prohibitive costs and its susceptibility to corruption make some reforms imperative."[30] As we all know, of course, everything moves slowly in the bureaucracy, and Egypt's civil servants have only had several millenia to work on the problem.

100

FOOTNOTES

1. E. H. Phelps Brown, "Guidelines for Growth and for Incomes in the United Kingdom: Some Possible Lessons for the United States," G. P. Schultz and R. Z. Aliber (eds.), *Guidelines, Informal Controls, and the Market Place* (Chicago: University of Chicago Press, 1966) p. 154.

2. *Newsweek*, September 8, 1952, p. 78.

3. David Smith, *Incomes Policy: Some Foreign Experiences and their Relevance for Canada* (Ottawa: Queen's Printer for the Economic Council of Canada, 1966) p. 123, Table 5-5.

4. *The Economist*, July 2, 1966, p. 15.

5. Eric Schiff, *Incomes Policies Abroad, Part 1* (Washington, D.C.: American Enterprise Institute, 1971) p. 11.

6. National Board for Prices and Incomes, *Productivity, Prices and Incomes for 1968 and 1969* (London: Her Majesty's Stationery Office) p. 3.

7. Eric Schiff, *op. cit.*, p. 11.

8. Eric Schiff, *Incomes Policies Abroad, Part 2* (Washington, D.C.: American Enterprise Institute, 1972) p. 7.

9. *Le Monde*, from *The Guardian* English section (London, October 3, 1976).

10. International Monetary Fund, *Staff Papers*, Vol. XX #1, March 1973, p. 172.

11. *Ibid.*, p. 173.

12. United Nations Economic Commission for Europe, *Incomes In Postwar Europe: A Study of Policies, Growth, and Distribution* (Geneva, 1967) Chapter 3, p. 4.

13. Schiff, *Incomes Policies Abroad, Part 1, op. cit.*, p. 19.

14. OECD Report by the Secretary General, *Inflation: the Present Problem*, December 1970, Annexes B, p. 88.

15. Arthur K. Okun, "The Controlled Experiment of 1969," Appendix to *Inflation, the Problems and Prospects Before Us* (Charles C. Moskowitz Lecture, 1970).

16. Congressman Philip M. Crane, "The Economic Stabilization Act," *Congressional Record*, December 9, 1971.

17. We are indebted to Donald L. Losman's article, "Inflation in Israel: The Failure of Wage-Price Controls," in *The Journal of Social and Political Studies*, Spring 1978, for many of the facts and figures in this section.

18. D. Patinkin, *Studies in Monetary Economics* (New York: Harper & Row, 1972) p. 78

19. Nadav Halevi and Ruth Klinov-Malul, *The Economic Development of Israel* (New York: Frederick A. Praeger, 1968) p. 258.

20. Alex Rubner, *The Economy of Israel* (New York: Frederick A. Praeger, 1960) p. 57.

21. Yoram Weiss, "Price Control in Israel," *Economic Review* (The Bank of Israel) March, 1971, p. 73.

22. Carol S. Greewald, "Price-Wage Controls: The Israeli Experience," *New England Economic Review* (Federal Reserve Bank of Boston) January-February 1972, p. 3.

23. *Ibid.*, p. 8.

24. Abba Lerner and Haim Ben-Shadar, *The Economics of Efficiency and Growth* (Cambridge: Ballinger Publishing Co., 1975) p. 96.

25. Donald L. Losman, *op. cit.*

26. Peter Samuel, "Much Ado About Nothing: The Australian Wage and Price Freeze, April 1977," in Sudha Shenoy (ed.) *Wage-Price Control: Myth and Reality* (Turramurra, Australia: The Centre for Independent Studies, 1978) pp. 254–55.

27. *The Washington Post*, January 30, 1977, p. A16.

28. *Ibid.*, April 29, 1978, p. A16. On page 10 of this book, we cited an historian who wrote about price controls in Egypt in 306 B.C. in these words: "There was a whole army of inspectors. There was nothing but inventories, censuses of men and animals. . ."

29. *Ibid.*, January 30, 1977, p. A16.

30. *Ibid.*

14

The Price of World Currency

When someone buys a share in a large corporation for $100, he is merely exchanging one commodity (money) for another (stock). Similarly, one international currency (say, dollars) can be exchanged for another (say, yen or sterling). The exchange rate between dollars and stock which buyer and seller agree on is the *price* of the share; the exchange rate between currencies is usually referred to only as the exchange rate, although in every way it is just like a price.

One of the key ways in which exchange rates are like prices is that governments strive to regulate them.

GOLD AND SILVER

Suppose that we have only two international currencies, gold and silver. Then there will be an exchange rate between them, since people are willing to exchange most things provided that they can agree on the rate of exchange.

In the Middle Ages, gold and silver circulated as media of exchange in exactly this way. Sometimes gold was the most common medium, sometimes silver. In the sixteenth century the new finds of silver in the New World gave silver the upper hand. But such inflows strained the accepted doctrine that silver had a "proper" gold price. In other words, price-fixing of silver against gold was subject to just the same pressures as any other attempt to fix prices.

Because of the so-called Gresham's Law,* named after the English Treasury Minister of the time:

> There was a tendency for one type of coin to become dominant when governments were willing to exchange silver for gold... [only] according to a specific standard. Under these conditions either the gold or silver coin could be expected to circulate less. If, for example, the free bullion market gave more silver for gold than the government standard for coinage at the government mint, the natural tendency would be to melt down gold coins and sell them for silver on the free market. On the other hand, if the free bullion market gave more gold for silver than the government mint, the tendency would be for gold to be coined while silver coins would be melted down for bullion to sell in the free market. . . . The "bad" money, that contained the metal less favored in the free market compared with the government standard, drove out the

* Bad money drives out good.

"good" money, that contained the metal more favored in the free market. Gresham's law was for centuries a *bete noire* to governments issuing bimetallic currencies, because as the market ratio between them would change, one currency would tend to move out of circulation.[1]

Price-fixing of one currency in terms of another just did not work.

In order to get around the problems of bimetallism, England started to quote prices in gold and also in silver, allowing the value of gold in terms of silver to vary, but the so-called "parallel standard" was an obvious inconvenience to trade and in 1717 it was abolished. And once more the official exchange rate of 15:20 did not correspond with the market rate. The official exchange of silver for gold was higher than the market rate and so silver tended to move out of circulation.

Again, market conditions changed, and the price trends eventually reversed, such that gold climbed in the 1781–1800 period to reach an exchange rate of 15.09, and seemed likely to move above the official rate. Had this been so, Gresham's law would have meant that silver would have been brought back into circulation and gold would have been pushed out. To prevent this, the British government had to stop the coinage of silver altogether, except for coins which were so "bad" (that is, had a silver content less than their face value) that they stayed in circulation.

Most of Europe remained on bimetallism, but this happy price-fixing was blotted by two developments in the mid-nineteenth century. The first was the rapid increase in gold production from California; the second was the absorption of all world silver production as currency in India. Hence, the market price of silver in Europe was pushed up and bimetallism was put under irresistible strains.

Strangely, the conventional wisdom in international currency markets was that a fixed rate of exchange between gold, silver and other (paper) currencies was the very foundation of stable world trade and prosperity. It is an understandable belief, but it was eventually shattered by the upheaval of the First World War. Exchange rates began to fluctuate, to be set at new levels, and then to fluctuate again. Britain fixed its currency in terms of the price of gold in 1925. But the pressure upon sterling (and upon most of the currencies of the belligerents) proved too much to withstand, and on September 21, 1931, Britain allowed the pound to float. Its value against the dollar declined 30 percent by the end of the year. Rolfe and Burtle write:[2]

> In most of the world, England's abandonment of the gold standard was viewed as an unprecedented disaster. But, freed of the burden of an unrealistic exchange rate, the economic results in England were favorable. Between 1931 and 1936, United Kingdom manufacturing production climbed 44.5 percent. Much less progress was made in countries that went back to the gold standard. England's floating rate was followed in 1934 by a dollar devalua-

tion in terms of gold (of 40.9 percent) and the gold bloc in an effort to retain their fixed parities was put under more and more strain.

BRETTON WOODS

The world powers meeting at Bretton Woods, New Hampshire, in 1944, developed a new system of international currency exchange, which fixed parities up to a point, but which never really worked. The gold exchange system was revived and gold became the foundation of the new economic system. Each nation would hold its reserves in gold, which could be freely converted into dollars. The parities of other currencies were fixed, but devaluation was possible within a narrow range of ten percent, more if there was agreement from the International Monetary Fund.

So, prices were fixed once again. But before Bretton Woods could work, huge depreciations against the dollar were necessary, and took place before 1950. This widespread suspension of the rules made the effectiveness of the whole agreement open to doubt and by 1958 it had become more evident that the system of fixed rates created massive disequilibria, huge and alarming flows of gold from the United States, and so on. Currencies reeled in 1965 as countries like Britain found they had to devalue against the dollar and Germany became the new financial power in Europe. The agreement was formally dissolved in 1971 when President Nixon ended the convertibility of the dollar into gold. Despite the fact that these devaluations and revaluations were regarded as a major defeat for the countries concerned and a major defeat for a system which they all wanted to succeed, they found that "the process designed to maintain international payments equilibrium or to restore it if it has been disturbed. . . [functioned] less and less effectively."[3] The professed objective of the agreement, "to promote exchange stability and exchange arrangements and to avoid competitive exchange depreciation,"[4] did not work. The theory of the value of fixed currency prices turned out to be an obsolete misconception.

FOOTNOTES

1. Sidney E. Rolfe and James Burtle, *The Great Wheel: The World Monetary System* (New York: Quadrangle/The New York Times Book Co., 1973) p. 4.

2. *Ibid.*, p. 31.

3. Tom De Vries, "Jamaica, or the Non-reform of the International Monetary System," *Foreign Affairs*, April 1976, Vol. 54, p. 578.

4. Van Merrhaege, *International Economic Institutions* (New York: St. Martin's Press 1971) p. 23.

15

The U.S., Britain and Canada: 1970–78

Two roughly parallel programs aimed at keeping down prices and wages were introduced on both sides of the Atlantic in the early seventies. The persons in charge of each of these programs must have had at least a few misgivings as they set out to tread a well-worn path. Milton Friedman had just written in *Newsweek* (on January 11, 1971) that

> The Johnson Administration tried wage-price guidelines. The guidelines failed and were abandoned. The British tried a wage-price board. It failed and has just been abolished. The Canadians tried voluntary wage-price controls. Their Prices and Incomes Commission recently announced the program was unworkable and would be abandoned January 1 [1971].

AMERICA'S PHASES

From August 15, 1971 through April 30, 1974, government officials in the United States attempted to suppress the rise in prices by imposing varying degrees of controls. During this period, the Wholesale Price Index (WPI), nevertheless, increased at an annual rate of 12.0 percent and the Consumer Price Index (CPI) increased at an annual rate of 7.2 percent. In contrast, during the twelve months before the start of the controls, WPI increased 3.3 percent per annum, and CPI increased at an annual rate of 4.3 percent. An observer from Mars could be forgiven for committing the fallacy of *post hoc ergo propter hoc* and suggesting that the price controls caused the inflation!

The initial Freeze was a surprise action aimed at avoiding strategic price and wage increases while a more sophisticated control program was formulated and implemented.

Just prior to the Freeze, the rate of inflation was running about 4.5 percent per annum; so after the end of a 90-day freeze the level of prices would be about one percentage point below the level that market forces would have produced if the market price level had continued to grow at about the same rate as previously. Even this is a high estimate of the difference between what we might call the "ceiling" and the "market" price levels, however. Since the growth rate of wages normally exceeds the growth rate of prices by the amount of productivity growth, a successful freeze on wages might cause the price level to fall over time. If this is to happen, the freeze on wages must not result in labor shortages. In fact, firms were able to hire increased quantities of labor at the frozen wage scales and employment grew at the rapid rate of 4.2 percent per annum from August to November 1971.[1]

Eventually Phase One came to an end, and Phase Two started on November 14, 1971. The object of the Price Commission (which was the regulatory agency) was to disallow all price increases except those justified by rising costs. The belief was that Phase Two controls would reduce the rate of increase in the general level of prices to about 2.5 percent per annum. In fact, Phase Two lasted until January 1973 and, during that time, the Wholesale Price Index increased at an annual rate of 6.4 percent and the Consumer Price Index increased at an annual rate of 3.4 percent.

Like the seasons, price control policies merge one into the other more quickly than we realize, and Phase Two gave way to Phase Three in January 1973. Here, the mandatory controls were replaced with voluntary controls. The goal for Phase Three was also to keep prices down to 2.5 percent, but having noted the ineffectiveness of the Phase Two policies, one might anticipate the effect of Phase Three. In fact, Phase Three also did not achieve its aim and, during the five months of its existence, WPI increased at an annual rate of 20.1, while CPI increased at an annual rate of 8.1 percent. Phase Three was a failure.

Despite this experience, President Nixon ordered a second price freeze on June 13, 1973. The freeze was to last for sixty days and controlled the prices of most commodities, as well as wages. There should, again, have been no increase in prices during those sixty days. In fact, prices increased at an annual rate of 5.0 (WPI) and 5.1 (CPI) percent.

It was an Administration of surprises and Phase Four controls were introduced on August 12, 1973; an unsuspecting America was again under mandatory price controls. The Secretary of the Treasury, George Schultz, stated that the goal of the Administration was to reduce price increases to three percent per annum or less. During the nine months of Phase Four, WPI went up at an annual rate of 18.3 percent, and the Consumer Price Index went up at an annual rate of 11.4 percent. Phase Four was the fifth failure of the program. The steady rise in prices was inexorable.[2]

So much for what controls did not do; now let us see what *did* happen. When the rate of inflation is corrected for quality deterioration during the period 1971–74, we see that the price level continued to rise at a very steady rate through the period of controls.[3]

Darby is skeptical of the overall effectiveness of the Economic Stabilization Program when it is considered in the longer run. He comments:

> From the second quarter of 1971 through the third quarter of 1975 the GNP deflator rose by 31.9 percent. Allowing for the usual lag of 1.5 years for price changes behind money supply changes, this is to be compared with a 31.0 percent increase in the money supply from the fourth quarter of 1969 to the first quarter of 1974.

108

Now the trend growth rate of the real quality of money demanded over the last several decades is between 0 and 0.5 percent per annum depending on the method of calculation used. So over 4.5 years the increase in the price level should be between 0 and 2 percentage points less than the increase in the money stock over the corresponding period. So the fact that the actual growth in prices *exceeded* that of money by 0.9 percentage points would indicate that the overall effect of the ESP on prices was either nil or to slightly increase them relative to what they otherwise would have been.[4]

It is startling that an economist of Darby's expertise and reputation could assert that the net effect of price controls could have been to *increase* prices. He also believes that there is no evidence that output was at all influenced by the program, contrary to the claims of the Administration at the time.

Congressman Steven Symms of Idaho (who opposed the Economic Stabilization Act) inserted into the *Congressional Record* a succinct analysis of the results of the Nixon program offered by the editor of *Barron's*, Mr. Robert Bleiberg, in a lecture at Hillsdale College, Michigan.

Representative Symms noted that

> The conclusion of Mr. Bleiberg's lecture may be summarized in one paragraph. He asked:
> What did wage and price controls achieve? Well, let's look at the record. In early May of 1972, Don Conlan, chief economist of the Wall Street brokerage firm of Dean Witter & Co., estimated that wholesale prices at the time were roughly where they would have been without controls. Projecting trends evident prior to August 15, 1971, he reckoned that the Wholesale Price Index in March of 1972 would have stood at 117.5% of the 1967 average. The actual figure was 117.4% observed Mr. Conlan. All that grief and confusion for one tenth of a percentage point improvement over free markets.[5]

The opposition to the Nixon program of wage and price controls cut across party lines, political philosophies and all economic classes. George Meany, the President of the American Federation of Labor and the Congress of Industrial Organizations strongly opposed controls,[6] as did Members of Congress, ranging from the conservative Republican Philip M. Crane[7] to the able chairman of the Republican Conference of the House of Representatives, generally regarded as a liberal leader, John Anderson.[8]

FROZEN MEAT PRICES

It would be fair to credit the United States government with some "success" in keeping the price of meat down during the period of the Economic Stabilization Program. This was an important issue, because the power of the American housewife cannot be overestimated, especially when she is angry, as many

American housewives were over the cost of meat. In response to this pressure, the Administration imposed ceiling prices on red meats in March 1973 and extended them in June 1973.

The disruption of supply was quite severe, at least for a short time. According to Brittan and Lilley, "The meat price ceilings and Freeze 2 produced much more dislocation and appearance of shortage than the public had anticipated. . . . The dismay at the disruption caused by Freeze 2 was so great that opinion switched round overnight against controls."[9]

Since the price of live steers continued to rise during the freeze, red meat dealers found themselves working on closer and closer margins; many small plants had to close their operations. By August, many retail chains were eliminating the middle-men who remained and were ordering custom slaughtering in an effort to accommodate demand. The price of live animals was once more bid up.

The effect of all this disruption was to make supplies of meat much more uncertain than in the previous year, fluctuating wildly throughout the period of the controls.

Nevertheless, the government held to a rigid price limitation on cattle products, despite the predictions of severe shortages (which were only partially evident on the butcher's block). The continuation of the policy was made possible by frequent and accurate information as to the state of the market. Quite simply, the Department of Agriculture received daily reports of the slaughter of food animals, and this enabled it to measure the intensity of the threatened beef shortage by the number of animals slaughtered that day. While supplies of beef became short, the meat was never completely inaccessible. Even so, the restrictions on price were quickly removed.

If the government, with daily information about the state of supplies, cannot hold down the price of essential items like beef, then its attempts to check price-rises in the whole economy, amongst products whose precise supply is uncertain at any particular moment, must be that much more difficult. There is no doubt that a substantial number of civil servants in the Department of Agriculture were working on the beef shortage full time; offices were humming, telephones ringing constantly throughout the length and breadth of the continent in order to ascertain daily supplies. It was a veritable triumph of modern government planning. But could it really have been worth the cost?[10]

AFTER THE NIXON CONTROLS

Since the foreclosure of the Nixon program in 1974, the scenario has been a mixture of threatening noises about the reintroduction of controls and a world slump that has been said to have been the worst since the Great Depression. Throughout 1974 and 1975 inflation fell rapidly in the U.S., but then an upsurge of output in 1977 renewed talks of controls with support coming from the most unlikely quarters. The Federal Reserve Bank of New York, previously a staunch

110

opponent of controls, suggested[11] that a wage and price policy may have a role in reducing inflationary expectations and cited Britain's renewal of controls as evidence of this. Opposition followed from the AFL-CIO in the figure of George Meany who stated, "We're very wary of wage and price controls."[12]

Carter also seemed to rule out controls upon his election to office but subsequent events showed his alternative "anti-inflation policy" to consist only of exhortations and budgetary recommendations wholly opposed to price stability. As inflation rose again in 1978 (at the rate of 10.1 percent in the second quarter), the congressional Joint Economic Committee recommended controls and Carter's opposition started to look less and less believable.

In the fall of 1978, most economic reporters and economists active in politics were predicting that the Carter Administration would soon unveil a new and stronger "anti-inflationary program" which would include "voluntary controls" especially for big business and big labor backed up by strong governmental "persuasion."

As early as the end of 1976, for instance, the economic columnist for *The Washington Post*, Hobart Rowen, wrote that "To make both goals—greater employment and control of inflation—compatible, fiscal and monetary policy must be supplemented by voluntary wage-price restraints—sometimes called "income policies."[13]

Ralph Nader, in a recent column, warned that ". . . should inflation remain at current or higher levels, Carter will find it difficult to avoid imposing a selective, mandatory price-wage control policy in . . . key industries."[14]

Dr. Herbert Stein, a former economic adviser to President Nixon (who reluctantly took part in the Nixon period controls), has flatly predicted that mandatory controls are likely in the near future.[15]

A leading economist with ties to the liberal Democrats, Dr. Robert Lekachman, recently asserted that "I agree with Stein that controls are in our near future." He added that "Unlike him, I consider them potentially benign, if they are appropriately designed and judiciously applied."[16]

And, of course, the talented novelist from Cambridge, Massachusetts, John Kenneth Galbraith (who has never been happier than when he was serving his country in the Office of Price Administration) chimes in periodically with the same advice.[17]

An important factor is that a majority of the people (a) regard inflation as the number one problem facing the country and (b) favor wage and price controls as a means of combatting it. According to the Gallup Poll of February 10-13, 1978, 44 percent of those polled favored controls while 40 percent were opposed. In a poll taken during April 14-17, the percentage favoring controls rose to 50 percent. More recent polls show that percentage nearing 60 percent.

On the other hand, the arguments against controls are so strong that many powerful voices within the liberal community still oppose them. *The Washington Post*'s lead editorial for July 27, 1978, for instance, offered a concise summary of why controls won't work.

111

With the current surge of inflation, the question of wage and price controls keeps bobbing up. Prices rose at an annual rate of 7.1 percent in the first three months of this year. But in the next three months, through June, it was up to 10.1 percent. Once again, food prices have been leading the way. Why not invoke controls again?

The answer is that they did serious damage the last time the country tried them, in 1971–73, and the effects are still visible. President Carter has flatly ruled out controls, and he's right. One reason is the adamant opposition of the labor unions, who learned that it is easier to control wages than prices. But the controls also conveyed other lessons that are worth recalling now. . . .

Controls do queer things to investment and production. Throughout the 1960s, oil and gas drilling slowly declined in this country. The turnaround came in 1972 when controls were in effect. The steel companies had regarded drilling pipe as a minor product.

They made it on aging equipment, and profit margins were low. When orders for new pipe began to pick up, the steel companies had little incentive to make more of it. The result was a wild scramble among drillers for pipe, and something very much like a black market appeared. Drilling costs shot upward much faster than the general inflation rate, and kept going even after controls expired. Moral: Price controls can sometimes be, paradoxically, more inflationary than no controls.

For consumers, it's the inflation in food prices that is the most immediately painful. But food prices are the hardest for a government to control. Housewives' demonstrations against the high cost of beef, in early 1973, induced the White House to put ceilings on meat prices. Some stock raisers held their animals off the market to wait out the controls. Others exported their cattle, mainly to Canada.

Two morals here: First, a country can't maintain price controls unless it is also prepared to curb exports, which in turn damages foreign markets and violates trade agreements. Second, controls create shortages. The disappearance of beef from the stores turned customers toward fish and poultry in such numbers that those were soon in shortage as well. At that point a lot of people began to fear a looming nationwide shortage of food in general. To head off a public panic, the administration was forced to drop the controls.

Controls are tolerable only for very short periods, in emergencies. The Carter administration knows that working down the current inflation is going to take a long, long time. It is relying mainly on exhortation, persuasion and, increasingly, cuts in federal spending. That isn't very dramatic, and it doesn't produce quick results. But it's better than the alternative.

VOLUNTARY CONTROLS UNDER CARTER

As many had predicted, on October 24, 1978, President Carter, in a televised address, announced his new program of voluntary wage and price controls. The President's aim is to hold inflation in the year ahead to a maximum of 5.75 percent. (On October 27, the Labor Department stated that, according to its statistics, consumer prices rose in September at an annual rate of 10 percent. Double-digit inflation had arrived.)

The Administration's guideline for wage increases was set at 7 percent. The limits on price increases are much more complicated, as befits the magnitude of the task the President is attempting. The absolute limit on price increases was set at 9.5 percent, no matter what the general rate of inflation turns out to be. The government's powers of persuasion coupled with its ability to influence big business through government contracts will be enlisted in the new war on inflation.

In a new proposal, President Carter said he would ask Congress to grant tax rebates to workers who abided by the 7 percent limit and were then hurt because of a rise in inflation over that figure. (Such a rise now seems likely.)[18]

The reaction of most unions was hostile. George Meany, the President of the AFL-CIO, in a concise letter to *The Washington Post* (November 3, 1978) clearly stated the position of most labor unions:

> The AFL-CIO's call for mandatory, across-the-board economic controls is not a public-relations maneuver . . . It is a carefully considered, completely responsible alternative to the ill-advised, inequitable program of the administration.
>
> Our proposal specifically rejected the same legislative route— the "blank check to the president"—that led to the Nixon package. It is precisely because we remember the 1971–73 disaster—and the World War II success—that we urge the Congress to draw up firm, comprehensive legislation based on equity and equal sacrifice.
>
> Such a program would by no means open the door to the pre-control inflationary price increases *The Post* predicts. We would expect that the Congress would thwart any inequitable price increases with a firm roll-back order and stop profiteering by an excess profits tax.
>
> Since we are convinced legislation is inevitable—and that is certainly the end result of the administration's program—we have stressed the need for immediate congressional action. We hope the president will reconsider his rejection of a special session of the Congress, so that America can get to work halting inflation, not just talking about it. And an open declaration of that intent by the president would clearly have the opposite effect to that envisioned by *The Post*.
>
> We don't like controls—mandatory or "voluntary." We want to

113

return to the free marketplace at the earliest possible moment. But there are worse things than controls. Recession is worse. Runaway inflation is worse. Discriminatory and unequal controls are worse. Scapegoating of wage-earners without due process is worse.

We see no possibility that anything short of full, fair, and equal controls on all segments of the economy will do the job. The actions on Wednesday to ensure sharp, inflationary increases in interest rates, with even graver danger of recession, heighten that need.

As this book went to press in late 1978, it was, of course, unclear what the future will bring. When Congress returns it will doubtless have before it several proposals for action, including the imposition of mandatory controls in 1979.

BRITAIN'S STAGES

Over the period 1972–1974, the government of the United Kingdom operated a wage and price stabilization program which was almost identical to that in the United States one year earlier and which was largely copied from it. Conservative Party Prime Minister Edward Heath introduced this program after the inflationary monetary expansion earlier in his government and learned a lesson which even Mr. Heath now acknowledges.

The policy was a major failure; it failed to stabilize prices and led only to a pressure from trade unions toward higher pay settlements which eventually toppled the government in 1974.

A strike by coal miners (who in the United Kingdom are all government employees) and its settlement led off a round of wage and price increases during the summer of 1972; in response the government imposed its pay freeze in November of that year. The effects of the freeze were fairly dramatic, although earnings (which included overtime and bonuses not covered by the regulations) were far from static.

There was a jump to almost 15 percent annual rate of increase in weekly earnings during Stage 2, despite the government target of 7.5 percent.[19]

During Stage 3 of the controls, the pay bill was expected to rise by about nine percent, but the actual average settlements of 9.1 percent and the average retail price index rise of 9.8 percent triggered a threshold agreement which pushed wages up further. This agreement had been negotiated with the unions by the government and allowed for an increase in weekly pay of 1.20 pounds for some ten million workers—plus regular adjustments in line with the cost of living.

Prices during the period of regulation were much influenced by external factors such as the oil crisis, which the government attempted to take into account and which weakened the apparent sanctions of the price rules. Even so, the huge increase in the inflation rate from 1970 onwards cannot be explained away so easily. The rate quickly rose to 15 percent during 1973 and at the end of

114

1976 was running at an annual rate of over 26 percent despite the maintenance of wage controls by the Labor government.

It might be significant that the money supply, measured in terms of a broad definition, M_3, expanded by about 25 percent in 1972 and 1973.[20]

Samuel Brittan and Peter Lilley have provided us with a perceptive commentary on the results of the Heath government's policies.

> . . . the major reason for Britain's propensity to experiment with incomes policy lies probably not in material performance but in its intellectual climate.
>
> The British opinion-forming classes—civil servants, politicians, commentators and academics—had largely stopped thinking in terms of the market mechanism. They felt much more at home with politically determined 'strategies'. Consequently the market was readily assumed to have 'failed' even when it was working, and when inflation did worsen this was always attributed to the inherent weaknesses of collective bargaining rather than to prior monetary excess. By contrast, the persistent failure of incomes policies has rarely been attributed to the inherent weaknesses of centrally administered systems of controlling prices and wages, but to some specific failure of administration, union sabotage or electoral cowardice which would not be repeated 'next time'.
>
> It is not only in Britain that incomes policies have failed. Neither in those democratic countries studied in detail in the previous chapters nor in other similar countries which have also experimented with incomes policies have such policies succeeded in suppressing inflation more than temporarily. Indeed, with the possible exception of the Netherlands, controls do not appear to have succeeded in restraining wages for much more than a year below the level they would have obtained in the absence of controls. Even such brief periods of restraint have been followed by wage explosions which have usually more than wiped out the temporary gain.
>
> Although incomes policies are often advocated to restrain so called 'cost-push' forces and then make it easier to bring monetary expansion under control, in practice incomes policies have not been so used. They have been used almost exclusively to suppress and delay the effect of previous monetary expansion on prices and wages. Even though the overall effect on the level of prices and wages has been minimal (outside the totalitarian states) the effect on the structure of relative prices has often led to serious distortions.[21]

The present Labor Government of Prime Minister James Callaghan seems to have learned something from recent experience. The Secretary of State for Prices and Consumer Protection Roy Hattersley (a moderate Labor MP) told an interviewer last December that there were certain prices he could control, but that he does not wish to control them. If he did do so, he commented, he would

115

be working against the greater good of economic prosperity. "I do not think an investment climate is there," he went on, "if there is a suspicion that every time prices go up a fraction more than I think right, there have to be questions. People won't take the risks of investment. The net result is lower profits, less investment, less employment."

He also pointed out that the cost of regulation of prices is very counter-productive: "It takes a great deal of statistical accounting work to supply the information that the Price Commission needs. I was told that one big company had people in their thousands working out the price code—as many as they had working on making the best of the tax laws. It doesn't seem to me that that is very productive."[22]

Perhaps there is still some hope that democratic socialists will realize what their Tory predecessors did not, namely that the major cause of inflation is government over-spending and that all the regulations of wages and prices in the world will not bring about economic health until the government sets its own house in order.

Britain's latest round of "incomes policy" commenced in August 1975 and consisted of a "pseudo-voluntary" guideline on wages and statutory limitations on price increases combined with gradual reductions in income tax.

The policy was enacted against a background of rapidly rising unemployment (to the highest postwar levels) and world slump. Inflation certainly fell during the time incomes policy was in force, but even traditional supporters of wage and price controls have been unable to attribute this to the government program. They point to the fact that the massive rise in unemployment and world slump has reduced union bargaining power, prevented firms from raising prices as demand sagged and lowered the cost of imported raw materials. At the time of this writing, inflation is expected to rise again before the end of the year (1978)[23], despite the fact that the British government is seeking an even lower guideline for wage increases. Monetary policy was also tighter in 1974–76 and this can be presumed to be the reason for much of the abatement in inflation. It is because of the recent increase in the money supply that most commentators expect inflation to rise again soon.

The 1977–78 ceiling on wage increases was 8–10 percent but the actual increases ran at 14 percent due to "wage drift." Union resistance to a "Stage 4" running through to mid-1979 is increasing.

At the annual Trades Union Congress in September of 1978, the unions turned down the Prime Minister's appeal to support his "Stage 4" wage limit of 5 percent.[24] Mr. Callaghan threatened to use monetary and fiscal policy to keep down the rate of inflation if the unions would not "voluntarily" support his limit. And so "incomes policy" in Britain staggers on, facing a double-digit inflation rate next year, with little cooperation from the powerful unions. It is unclear exactly what form future wage and price controls will take, but it is a good bet that they will be around in Britain for some time to come.

116

CANADA: THE LATE ENTRY

As if North America had not only recently learned its lesson, the Canadian Prime Minister Pierre Trudeau asked his parliament to impose wage and price controls in October 1975. The ceiling on wage increases that he wanted was a fairly high one, ten percent or $2,400, whichever was the lower.

In the final version of the Canadian controls, adopted in 1976, wage increases were limited to 14 percent and fines were levied for noncompliance. Irving Pulp and Paper was fined for its grant of a 23 percent increase in wages.

It may be noted that Canadian businessmen are not the only ones finding wage and price controls difficult to bear. In November 1976, Canadian workers participated in a general strike to protest the government's program. A day of strikes and demonstrations was called by the giant Canadian Labor Congress in an effort to persuade the government of Pierre Trudeau to repeal all the controls or at least to curtail them before their schedules expire in 1978. The opposition of ordinary workers to wage and price controls can be seen in many countries—Canada, the United States and Great Britain being the most prominent recent examples. Yet these workers are presumably the very people whom controls are supposed to help.

A newly-founded center for economic research in Canada, the Fraser Institute, which has already built up a considerable reputation for its scholarly publications, analyzed the recent history and probable consequences of Canadian controls soon after they were imposed.[25] Michael Walker, their editor, noted that there is little likelihood that the controls which then afflicted his nation would have any substantially different result than all the others of the past centuries.

Canadian controls followed two years of double-digit inflation which was running close to 11 percent by the time the controls were introduced. They consisted of a three year program to limit wages to 12 percent, 10 percent, and 6 percent rises in 1976, 1977, and 1978 respectively and profit margins were constrained to 95 percent of the average in the five years before controls. These restraints applied only to those in companies with more than 500 employees and thus covered only half the Canadian work force.

Initially, price increases fell to half their pre-controls levels (from 10.6 percent to 5.6 percent) within a year of the start of the program and this naturally led politicians to start praising the efficacy of their anti-inflation program. In fact, the chief economist of Toronto Dominion Bank was nearer the mark when he said that much of the improvement in Canada's price performance cannot be attributed to controls since foodstuffs were not subject to the controls and their prices declined.[26]

Since then the rate of inflation has risen to 8 percent in 1977 and still higher in 1978.

The deleterious effects of the policy have been far more obvious. Strikes and walkouts have increased, unions and management have joined forces to outwit

117

the government, construction has fallen to record lows and capital spending by industry has plunged. J. Peter Gordon, Chairman and Chief Executive of Steel Company of Canada, says, "We have got to stop to adjust the economy. It should be lights out, immediate abandonment."[27]

Patrick Wallace of *The Wall Street Journal*'s Toronto Bureau noted that "Many economists . . . say controls not only are having little effect on inflation, but threaten to leave the Canadian economy a shambles."[28]

Richard G. Lipsey of Queen's University, writing in *Canadian Public Policy*, summed up the recent Canadian experience as follows:

> It is important to note that the harmful effects of controls are *quite independent* of the monetary and fiscal policies that accompany them. The effects follow directly from the impact of particular types of government intervention on the economy, the economic changes that this impact creates, and the durability of these changes. There is, therefore, no more reason to be sanguine about the harmful long-term effects of repeated applications of controls when they are instituted along with sensible monetary and fiscal policies (as appears to be the case in Canada) than when they are accompanied by self-defeating monetary and fiscal policies (as was often the case in Britain). My main message then is as follows. Wage-price controls are shown by economic theory, and demonstrated by an enormous wealth of factual evidence, to have no permanent effect on the price level. If these controls are never repeated in Canada, the long-term effects of this one attempt are not likely to be too serious. There are forces, however, that will be at work to cause the experiment to be repeated. If this does happen, then the time for alarm will already have passed. If these forces for repetition are to be resisted, and the long-term consequences are not to occur, then an appreciation of the long-term effects of repeated controls policies are needed in Canada now.
>
> I say, therefore, that *now* is the time to stand up and be counted. Now is the time to say loudly and clearly that wage-price controls are ineffective in their main objective and extremely harmful in all of their other effects.[29]

In April of 1978, Canada's wage and price controls were officially abandoned, although the wages of many workers will be held down if their contracts were negotiated during the controls period.[30] (For this reason, many trade unionists in both the U.S. and Canada have been talking about one year rather than three year contracts.) It was about last April that many people in the United States started to seriously consider bringing back controls. And so it goes.

FOOTNOTES

1. Michael R. Darby, "The U.S. Economic Stabilization Program of 1971–1974," in Michael Walker (ed.), *The Illusion of Wage and Price Control* (Vancouver, Canada: The Fraser Institute, 1976) pp. 136–37.

2. For more facts and figures on President Nixon's "Phases" see, besides the chapter by Michael R. Darby cited above, Samuel Brittan and Peter Lilley, *The Delusion of Incomes Policy* (London: Temple Smith, 1977) pp. 136–51.

3. Darby, *op. cit.*, p. 152.

4. *Ibid.*, p. 155.

5. *Congressional Record*, August 14, 1974, p. E5498.

6. See, for instance, "Business, Labor Join to Scrap Controls," *Human Events*, January 19, 1974, p. 1.

7. See Philip M. Crane, "The Economic Stabilization Act," *Congressional Record*, December 9, 1971.

8. See John Anderson, "The Cost of Controls," *The Ripon Forum*, April 1, 1974; and "Wage and Price Controls Are Not the Answer," position paper of the Business Roundtable, Washington, D.C., January 7, 1975.
   In addition, the president of the Chamber of Commerce of the United States, Arch N. Booth, wrote a tract entitled *Wage-Price Controls: The Challenge to Learn From History* (Washington, D.C., undated but published about 1975). The Chamber also published about the same time a booklet entitled *Wage and Price Controls: A Failure in History, Theory and Practice*.

9. Samuel Brittan and Peter Lilley, *op. cit.*, p. 145.

10. For an inside account of just how controls work (or don't work) see Jackson Grayson with Louis Neeb, *Confessions of a Price Controller* (New York: Dow-Jones Irwin, 1974). See also Mark Skousen, *Playing the Price Controls Game* (New Rochelle, N.Y.: Arlington House, 1977).

11. See *The Wall Street Journal*, March 1, 1978.

12. See *The New York Times*, November 11, 1976.

13. *The Washington Post*, December 12, 1976, p. M1.

14. *The Washington Star*, June 17, 1978, p. B2.

15. An excellent summary of the situation as of October 1, 1978 was published in *The Washington Post* that day (p. M3) by Art Pine. Mr. Pine quotes Dr. Stein's prediction and agrees with it.
    Dr. Stein, by the way, has collaborated with his son, Benjamin Stein, to write a fascinating novel about a Weimar-style inflation which overtakes the U.S. in the near future. Entitled *On the Brink*, it is published by Simon and Schuster (New York, 1977).

16. Robert Lekachman, "The Case for Controls," *The New Republic*, October 14, 1978, p. 18. For balance, see also one of the best critiques of the Nixon controls, Alan Reynolds' incisive article, "The Case Against Wage and Price Control," *National Review*, September 24, 1971.

17. See Tom Wicker's column (*The New York Times*, July 4, 1978) for a summary of Dr. Galbraith's views.

18. *U.S. News and World Report*, November 6, 1978, pp. 17–22.

19. For a good account of the Heath controls, see Michael Parkin, "Wage and Price Controls: The Lessons From Britain," in Michael Walker (ed.), *The Illusion of Wage and Price Control* (Vancouver, Canada: The Fraser Institute, 1976). See also Samuel Brittan and Peter Lilley, *The Delusion of Incomes Policy* (London: Temple Smith, 1977), especially pp. 152–183. Stephen Eyres, the managing editor of *The Free Nation* has written a somewhat critical review of the Heath incomes policies under the title "The Fatal Temptation." See *The Free Nation* (published by the National Association for Freedom, London) September 3, 1976.

20. Brittan and Lilley, *op. cit.*, p. 169.

21. *Ibid.*, pp. 178–180.

22. Elisabeth Dunn, "To the Manner Born," *The Spectator*, December 18, 1976, p. 14.

23. *The Economist* of London predicts a 10 percent rate of inflation at the beginning of next year; see its issue for September 9, 1978, p. 15.

24. *The Daily Telegraph*, October 4, 1978, p. 1 and editorial page.

25. See Michael Walker (ed.), *The Illusion of Price and Wage Control* (Vancouver, Canada: The Fraser Institute, 1976).

26. Quoted in Patrick Wallace, "Canada's Wage and Price Controls," *The Wall Street Journal*, July 29, 1977.

27. *Ibid.*

28. *Ibid.*

29. Richard G. Lipsey, "Wage-Price Controls: How To Do a Lot of Harm by Trying To Do a Little Good," *Canadian Public Policy*, Winter 1977, p. 12. For a more sympathetic view of Canadian controls, see Hobart Rowen, "Canada's Wage-Price Controls Achieve a Modest Success," *The Washington Post*, May 26, 1976, p. A14.

30. For a useful discussion of the recent Canadian experience under controls, see the anthology edited by Michael Walker, *Which Way Ahead: Canada after Wage and Price Control* (Vancouver, Canada: The Fraser Institute, 1977).

    The current status of wage and price controls in Europe, Japan and Canada (both voluntary and mandatory) is concisely summarized in *U.S. News and World Report*, November 20, 1978, p. 74. The headline ("Wage-Price Guidelines Abroad—Not Much Encouragement for U.S.") tells the story.

16

On the Causes of Inflation

Before a policymaker jumps to the conclusion that wage and price controls can actually *cure* an inflation, he should make an attempt to understand the true *causes* of that phenomenon. The absence of such understanding is one of the reasons that wage and price controls have had such a long and painful history of failure and ineffectiveness; controls may be able to suppress the *symptoms* of inflation, but the evidence shows that they are not a cure for the disease itself.

The underlying conditions necessary for inflation to occur are not really in dispute by economists and can therefore be thought of as the fundamental causes of inflation. Other economic factors contribute to an inflation, however, not only by putting a pressure on governments to continue inflationary expansions, but by spreading the inflation through the economy. Hence, some economists believe that these supplemental factors are just as important as the underlying conditions.

The underlying conditions can be described as follows:

(1) When aggregate expenditures expand faster than the increase in the supply of goods and services, the expansion allows and encourages a rising price level. Prices are, if you like, bid up to absorb the increase in aggregate expenditures.

(2) The expansion in aggregate demand can be generated by increased government spending or by a cyclical upswing in private demand. Again, where this expansion is greater than the expansion in commodity supply, a rising price level will be supported.

(3) These increases in demand and expenditure can occur only when the supply of money in the economy is larger than the demand for money balances. When this is so, the excess money will go into producing excess aggregate demand, assuming that the supply of commodities does not expand in step with the monetary increase. The necessity of this condition of monetary expansion to inflation is one of the reasons that has led the distinguished Nobel Prize-winning economist Milton Friedman to say that "Inflation is always and everywhere a monetary phenomenon."

Friedman himself cites an impressive correlation between the excess of money supply over output and inflation.[1] He has made the same point in numerous books and articles, but an analysis of the empirical testing of this theory is beyond the scope of the present work.

OTHER INFLATIONARY PRESSURES

Although monetary expansion is the ultimate necessary condition that allows an inflation to occur, it is, as has been said, not the only factor that constitutes a pressure toward inflation. Other economic factors, prompting increases in demand and excess money supply, contribute to inflation and allow it to spread quickly through the economy, making inflation politically difficult to deal with.

These other economic factors can be broadly summarized as follows:

(1) *Failure of prices to adjust in recession*

According to Phillip Cagan, who has extensively studied the movement of prices during boom and recession over the course of this century, "The distinctive feature of the postwar inflations has not been that prices rose faster in periods of cyclical expansion—many previous expansions had much higher rates—but that they declined hardly at all, or even rose, in recessions."[2] As an example of this in one industry, he cites the familiar example of the steel industry, in which from 1955 to 1960 the wholesale price index of iron and steel rose 21 percent while the index of all wholesale prices rose 8 percent. Over the same period, steel output *fell* 22 percent and capacity utilization was down to about 80 percent after 1955 and even lower during the subsequent strikes and recessions.

Such failure of prices to fall during a recession has been typical of the postwar economy, although the steel industry is a particularly emphatic example. Nevertheless, the coexistence of high rates of inflation with high rates of unemployment and recession has caused the public to be more and more aware of the phenomena of "stagflation" and "slumpflation."

(2) *Causes of the failure to adjust*

This effect—the failure of prices to adjust downward in a recession—has many causes. The first would be the downward inflexibility of wages and (to some extent) prices. A recession rarely comes suddenly, but is a slow process, occurring over a period of months or even years. Often the recession will be accompanied by government assurances that the recession is only temporary, or does not exist at all. Workers are, therefore, tempted to believe that the economic situation does not warrant a cut in salaries or a reduction in employment and will militate against any such suggestion. Furthermore, since recession is typified by an initial cutback in demand rather than falling prices, workers will object that they are being asked to accept cuts even though prices have not fallen. Their failure to take wage cuts will itself (since prices are fixed largely upon production costs, which include the price of labor) tend to prevent prices from falling.

Furthermore, industries tend to build up inventories during recession, rather than lay off men and underutilize equipment, both of which are painful decisions to make. This has the effect of drawing some part of supply off the market, thus keeping up prices, even though large stockpiles may be accumulated. Short-run shifts in demand can be absorbed and price fluctuations are, therefore, smaller.

As has been said, some industries find that it is costly to change their prices. The preparation of new price lists, new labelling and the administrative costs associated with these are one source of such costs. Price-cutting wars are another cost that large firms wish to avoid; hence the fact that the most concentrated industries (in which the first few firms have large percentages of the total industry sales) display a lower amplitude of cyclical price changes.[3] The further assumption by firms that the recession will soon be over (an assumption probably encouraged by optimistic government officials) will also discourage them from lowering their prices for what they perceive as a short period.

Although prices in the long run may adjust to meet changes in demand, there is no guarantee that short-run price changes will adjust. Wage rates are slow to adjust in a deceleration of inflation, as are service prices (which are closely related to wage rates), so there is little opportunity for prices to be diminished because of the importance of these costs in determining selling price. Firms may trim costs, use space and workers more efficiently, or cut out unprofitable products in favor of more profitable ones. In addition to these adjustments, the fact that most plants are designed to work most efficiently at a certain level of output means that average unit costs rise when production is cut back in the face of falling demand. This is yet another factor that tends to keep prices up during a depression, since prices are largely determined by costs.

(3) *Economic rigidities*

Inflation is perpetuated and spread through the reluctance of governments to change the existing economic institutions. Consequently, inflation is often allowed to continue, even though a small change in the existing economic structure would dissipate it. For instance, the major gold discoveries of 1849 served to expand the money supplies of the gold-standard countries, so that prices were pulled up in the 1850s and 1860s. The same phenomenon has been seen with respect to other currency metals at other times throughout history. If countries had merely abandoned their gold convertibility into gold and allowed their currencies to float in value against others, this inflationary effect could have been avoided. The fixed exchange rate, in conjunction with an expansion in specie reserves, actually serves to engender inflation in those countries subject to the fixed-rate agreement.

Another example is afforded by the common postwar policy of interest rate manipulation, particularly the attempts by the governments on both sides of the Atlantic to keep the interest rate down so that small borrowers would be able to afford loans. This policy, however, made it impossible for monetary restraint to be exercised through the usual device of selling low-price (and therefore high rate) Treasury securities on the open market. On the contrary, the interest rate policy required the Federal Reserve to *buy* securities in order to keep buying prices high and, therefore, interest rates low.

Still another policy objective that conflicts with anti-inflation policy is that of employment. It has long been thought that there is an approximate trade-off between inflation and unemployment; the larger the dose of inflation permitted in an economy, the smaller the rate of unemployment. Postwar policy has laid such emphasis on full employment that high rates of inflation have been accepted, but it seems to be an unfortunate fact (which will be examined in the next chapter) that larger and larger doses of inflation are needed to sustain a given employment level.

(4) *Expansions caused by war*

In the United States there have been four major economic expansions associated with high rates of inflation. Of these, all except the 1950s, "investment boom" years followed wars. There was a strong expansion of aggregate demand in World War II, although the inflationary effect of this was partly submerged in wage and price controls. Upon their removal in 1946, prices rose significantly and continued to rise until the end of 1948. The outbreak of the Korean War also had a severe inflationary effect, since a great deal of "scare buying" (partly due to fear of the reimposition of economic controls!) constituted a rise in aggregate demand in addition to the demands of the war itself. Prices in 1950 once again increased significantly. The escalation of the Vietnam War is also associated with a steady rise in the rate of inflation, although the rate did not fall to zero as the demand pressure eased; the phenomenon of the downward inflexibility of prices and of the now familiar "slumpflation" had begun to be noticeable.

The inflationary aspect of wartime expansions seems to suggest that this, and presumably more modest political policies, can have a marked effect on inflation. The goodwill of governments has not been sufficient to administer the monetary correction needed following these expansionary events, partly because of the rigidities in prices and wages that have been referred to. Noneconomic objectives, then, can interfere with our economic targets.

(5) *The advantage to governments*

Governments find many advantages in a mild inflation. Inflation is, in Friedman's words, "irresistibly attractive to sovereigns because it is a hidden tax that at first appears painless or even pleasant, and above all because it is a tax that can be imposed without specific legislation."[4] According to the same author (in *Essays on Inflation and Indexation*) government directly "profits" from inflation in three ways.

First, the additional government-created money will pay debts and finance expenditures over and above what the government collects in revenue.

Secondly, government-induced inflation pushes taxpayers into higher income brackets and thus leads to taxpayers paying *unlegislated* tax increases. According to the congressional Joint Committee on Internal Revenue Taxation, the real

124

income tax increase in 1974 caused by inflation totaled $7,122,000,000—a percentage increase of 5.9 for the average taxpayer. Since these statistics were compiled, the situation has become even worse. In 1953, the average family income was $5,000 and 11.8 percent of that was paid in direct taxes of all kinds—federal, state and local; according to the Advisory Commission on Intergovernmental Relations, the average family income in 1975 had risen to $14,000, but that family was paying 22.7 percent of its income in taxes—almost twice the amount paid two decades earlier. If we assume an annual inflation rate of six percent (a conservative assumption in a year when inflation is approaching the double-digit level), inflation-induced tax increases could net the federal government an additional unlegislated bonanza of $50 billion by 1980.[5]

Thirdly, the real amount of the national debt is reduced since the money had been borrowed at a time when the inflation rate was lower and money was worth more. Taking all these factors into account, Friedman estimates that the federal government's revenue from inflation came to more than $25 billion in 1973 alone.

Given these facts and figures, it will come as no surprise if the enthusiasm of at least many government officials for fighting inflation is less than all-consuming.[6]

Some other advantages of inflation should not be overlooked. The first is that an inflationary situation offers an opportunity for wages to be adjusted down in real terms even though no apparent decrease occurs. Given the downward inflexibility of wages, some economists thought that a mild inflation would actually benefit particular industries in their economic adjustment following reductions in demand. The second is that an inflationary expansion does call forth an increased supply in the short-term at least; employment is stimulated, and commerce prospers. Ending the inflation would mean a decline in employment, or wages, and the capitulation of firms that are only marginally profitable and can exist only under inflationary conditions. For governments, this prospect has not been appealing politically.

The phenomenon of inflation is therefore seen to have one major cause, but is associated with a large number of economic conditions, institutional rigidities and so on, which make simple solutions like wage and price controls inadequate as a cure.

FOOTNOTES

1. *Newsweek*, June 24, 1974.

2. Phillip Cagan, *The Hydra-Headed Monster* (Washington, D.C.: American Enterprise Institute, 1974) p. 3.

3. See James Tobin, "Inflation and Unemployment," Presidential Address to the American Economic Association, *American Economic Review*, Vol. 62, March 1972. See also Phillip Cagan, "Changes in the Recession Behavior of Wholesale Prices in the 1920s

and Post World War II," *Explorations in Economic Research* (New York: N.B.E.R., Winter 1975). See also W. F. Mueller, "Industrial Concentration: An Important Inflationary Force?", Paper presented at Columbia Law School Conference, March 1974, on *Industrial Concentration: The Economic Issues*.

4. Milton Friedman, "Using Escalators to Help Fight Inflation," *Fortune*, July 1974, p. 94.

5. For more information, see Donald J. Senese, *Indexing the Inflationary Impact of Taxes* (Washington, D.C.: The Heritage Foundation, 1978).

6. It must be remembered that inflation does have a constituency; while it clearly hurts certain groups in society (especially those living on fixed incomes) it benefits (at least in the short run) certain other groups, especially those who can use their economic or political power to "stay ahead" of inflation.

17

Coping With Inflation

Before jumping to conclusions about the cure for inflation, it is important to understand its cause. The lack of such an understanding explains why price and wage controls have had such a painful and ineffective history.

There is growing support for the hypothesis that inflation is always and everywhere a monetary phenomenon, caused principally by an expansion of the supply of money in circulation over and above the level of output. The mechanism by which such an expansion produces inflation is really quite simple.

If an expansion in the total supply of money which is in people's pockets and bank accounts happens to occur, but there is no corresponding expansion in industrial output, then it is natural that people will tend to spend a bit more. They might become less price conscious; they might tend to buy more expensive or better quality commodities; they might expand the number of goods and services which they buy. In any case, the effect will be the same: shopkeepers will find their prices being bid up—people will be prepared to pay more and to keep supply in line with demand; shops will raise their prices slightly. Wholesalers, many of whom sell their wares by auction, will find the same effects although they are powerless to stop them—prices will simply be bid higher. An expansion of the supply of money in circulation, without a corresponding expansion of the commodities in circulation will, therefore, produce a general rise in prices throughout the economy.

WHY GOVERNMENTS CAUSE INFLATION

Inflation can be caused in many ways. Perhaps the most obvious way occurs when the government spends in excess of the tax revenue it takes in. The money to pay for public programs has to come from somewhere and governments have a number of ways of getting new money into circulation.

One way would be to buy stocks from commercial customers or even to sell short-term stocks and bonds at high rates of interest. Another way is simply to take on more government employees and make sure that they are paid. In any of these circumstances, the new money gets into the economy because of government action—the government has to print new banknotes, mint new coin, and extend new credit.

There are, of course, many pressures on the government to inflate the money stock. It may be that the pressures from public employees for higher wages are irresistible. It might be that the government believes it is "fine-tuning" the economy and that prices will not really be raised by a modest inflation. It might be that the government wishes to stimulate the economy, believing that higher prices will produce more output (remember Say's law that supply produces its own demand; this is the exact reverse). It might be that industries find their margins tight because of union pressure for wage and working condition improvements, and so they sell stock, which the government buys, to compensate. There may be an infinite number of reasons. Ultimately, however, the government and its agencies are the root cause.

Some self-interested motives of the government should not be overlooked. An inflationary situation brings about more wage bargaining and higher average wages, so people find themselves moving into higher tax brackets. The government draws in more revenue and the people are powerless to prevent the erosion of their real earnings.

Furthermore, ending an inflation with strict monetary policy is not easy, because the "tight" monetary situation will undoubtedly mean that some firms will find that they can no longer exist in the market and will have to close down. Unemployment will be a result, at least in the shorter term.

THE PROBLEMS OF INFLATION

In fact, of course, inflation produces more unemployment the longer it continues. As the rate of inflation rises, more and more industries find themselves squeezed by a tight money situation and more workers are laid off.

But inflation itself produces a kind of unemployment—an underemployment of resources. This is because under inflation, it is very hard for people to predict the future: What price will stocks be a year from now? Will consumer preferences still be the same or will they have moved to cheaper varieties of goods? What will the labor unions bargain for at the next round of pay talks? These things produce uncertainty, and uncertainty produces an unwillingness to invest and doubt produces a misinvestment in unprofitable and underproductive industries.

Now we see why the traditional policy of wage and price controls cannot contain inflation. It is not a question of people deliberately raising their prices; it is a question of people being unable to accommodate a monetary situation which is not of their own making.

Take the owner of a grocery store. You might go in and find that the price of bread has risen by ten percent over the last month. You will chastise the owner of the store because of the price rise. But he will not accept any criticism; he will undoubtedly say that he is merely passing on a price rise from the wholesaler. Ask the wholesaler why his prices have risen; he will probably blame it on the baker; and the baker, on the miller. The miller will explain that the price rise is not of his own making, but comes directly from the farmer. The farmer will say that he cannot help but raise his prices, because this present inflation is making his farmhands less well off and they have pressed him for higher wage settlements.

None of them accepts the blame because none of them is blameworthy. They are merely trying to maintain their positions in an inflationary economy. Controls upon one part of the chain—say the retail price of bread—will jeopardize the welfare of the grocer because he will find his costs increasing all the time. Controls upon the whole cycle will leave everyone disgruntled, thinking that they are "behind the general trend." As we have seen over the history of the past fifty centuries, these problems are insuperable.

The ultimate cure, then, must be at the source of the inflation: a contraction in the supply of money per unit of output. But this is very painful; how can it best be cushioned?

INDEXATION

Perhaps the first priority is a major, if gradual, cut in public expenditures; government spending and administration must be brought in line with taxes if monetary equilibrium is to be restored to the inflationary economy. To a very minor degree, wage controls might have a short-term, "cosmetic" importance in reducing the expectations of price rises, lowering the marginal propensity of individuals to consume, and preparing the country for cuts in government services.

A proposal deserving serious consideration is comprehensive indexation. In this process, all contracts would be adjusted to make allowance for the prevailing rate of inflation, so that everyone knows where they actually are and nobody tends to "overbid" for inflation—which just forces the government to produce more inflation. (For example, in wage bargaining in the inflationary economy, unions bargain not only for the money which they have lost through inflation, but also for an amount that they expect to lose in the next contract period. This can only squeeze firms harder and thus pressure the government to come to their assistance with more expansionary measures.) As Milton Friedman says[1] of this proposal, one of the first things it would do is "temper some of the hardships and distortions that now follow from . . . inflation. Employers will not be stuck with excessively high wage increases. . . .Borrowers will not be stuck with excessively high interest costs, for the rates on outstanding loans will moderate as inflation recedes . . . . Businesses will be able to borrow funds or enter into construction contracts knowing that interest rates and contract prices will be adjusted later in accord with indexes of prices."

The mechanism of this indexation is simple. Cost-of-living agreements built into all wage bargains would insure the unions against future inflation and would lead to a real lowering of present settlement standards. This is so because "Without escalator clauses, a proportion of negotiated wage increases are simply a compensation for expected increases in the price level. However, once

129

negotiated, they must be paid, regardless of what actually happens to prices."[2] By getting rid of the over-expectation, indexed cost-of-living agreements reduce the pressure on the government to continue the inflation.

There is a strong case for a government guarantee that bonds—particularly bonds issued to small savers (who suffer more than most from inflation)—should have a built-in escalator clause. If this were the case, more certainty would be possible in investment and the productive capacity of industry would be increased. More output would help absorb the inflation.

Such an approach would make coping with inflation less painful, although a certain amount of painful reallocation is always necessary after a period in which investment has been low or has been uncertain and inefficient. But one thing is certain: unless backed up with a policy of this nature, no amount of wage and price control will stem the tide of inflation.

FOOTNOTES

1. Milton Friedman, "Monetary Correction," *Essays on Inflation and Indexation* (Washington, D.C.: American Enterprise Institute, 1974) p. 43.

2. David Laidler, "An Alternative to Price Controls," *The Illusion of Wage and Price Control* (Vancouver: The Fraser Institute, 1976) p. 207.

18

The Cures For Inflation

So far it has been shown that throughout history, wage and price controls have been ineffective as cures for inflation. Occasionally, they have relieved the symptoms of inflation for a while; sometimes, they have reduced expectations of inflation and therefore contributed to a reduction in the public pressure on the government to stimulate monetary growth. Always, however, they have been short-lived and they have never been fully effective in their nominated ends. Indeed, as has been pointed out, wage and price controls often have such a perverse effect on the economy that they worsen the inflationary situation. If wage and price controls are ineffective as cures, what measures are left? This chapter will review a few possibilities.

Earlier postwar economic theory recognized a phenomenon associated with the name of the economist, A. W. Phillips. This phenomenon was a negative correlation between the level of unemployment and the rate of change of money wages. According to this theory, wages would increase at a faster rate when unemployment was low and would increase at a slower rate (or even fall) when unemployment increased. If the assumption were made (and it is a reasonable assumption) that prices are linked to wages, then the "Phillips Curve" would suggest a stable negative correlation between the rate of change of prices and the level of unemployment.

At the time when the Phillips Curve analysis was being formulated, the rate of change of wages was small, despite some rather large short-term fluctuations. The relationship between unemployment and inflation seemed sufficiently stable under these conditions that it suggested a policy trade-off, perhaps inevitable, between unemployment and inflation. Policymakers could choose either a high level of employment, conjoined with a high level of inflation or they could cut down on their policies of economic stimulation and enjoy lower rates of inflation, albeit with higher unemployment rates. Even deflation was possible if aggregate demand, and hence employment, were sufficiently low. The position that a government adopted along the Phillips Curve was thought to depend entirely upon its policies, monetary, fiscal or other, to stimulate aggregate demand, and therefore employment.

Economists began to search for the numerical relationship between inflation and unemployment in a number of countries. Over time, however, it became clear that there was in fact *no* stable and negative correlation. At the postwar "full employment" rates, higher and higher rates of inflation seemed to be possible. The same level of employment apparently required an increasing degree of inflationary economic stimulation.

Milton Friedman, in his Nobel Prize acceptance speech, compared the employment rates with the rate of change of prices (after a short lag to accommodate the period necessary for price rises to work through after wages are increased) and found that the Phillips relation did indeed tend to be negative until the 60s, but after that, unemployment and inflation increased together. An exception is the United States, where the relation did not become positive until about 1973, which might explain why leading economists and world policymakers were so slow in accepting the turnaround, preferring to attribute it to special factors (trade union militancy, for instance) in each country. Nevertheless, as the 70s dawned, it became clear that "stagflation" was not only possible, but characteristic of many Western economies. It is as if the Phillips Curve *itself* has moved outward.

Why has this happened? In Friedman's view, it is *surprises* that matter; a 20 percent inflation rate could very well be accompanied by low unemployment rates, provided that it was constant and predictable. He says:

> An unanticipated change is very different. Firstly, the unpredictability of prices will make it difficult for producers to invest rationally, will generate doubt and uncertainty. Hiring will therefore tend to be diminished. Secondly, a volatile price level shortens the optimum length of unindexed labor commitments. In a volatile situation, employers will be much less likely to hire labor for a long period at a fixed wage, because of the risks that prices will fall while wages and other costs will continue to rise. An adverse effect on employment will be the result.

Furthermore, the effect of controls will confuse market prices and performance even further, as has already been explained. Governments set prices for a wide range of services—postal services, energy, and many more—and regulate even more. Under inflation, they take it upon themselves to control nearly all prices, either by explicit controls or by "voluntary" restraint. The resulting inability of the price system to guide economic activity leaves a given level of inflation compatible with rising unemployment. If employment becomes the principal end of government policy, then inflation could rise higher and higher. The old policy trade-off no longer operates. As Cagan says, "Policy makers face a dilemma. Inflation can be stopped, but the traditional policies work less effectively, and the nation has become more reluctant to incur the costs of using them forcefully. Hence doubt of the nation's ability to control inflation deepens, thus weakening price responses and, in turn, the effectiveness of policy restraint. Thus does inflation feed on its own strength."[1]

132

FIGHTING INFLATION BY 'INDEXING'

Governments are under considerable pressure to maintain an inflationary expansion. Employers who granted large wage increases in the expectation of continued inflation and borrowers who borrowed at high rates for the same reason would be in dire straits if an inflation were suddenly stopped. Furthermore, the government itself benefits from inflation, as has been noted. The problem of curing inflation is therefore reduced to the problem of finding ways in which this pressure upon the government can be reduced.

One particularly promising approach is the concept of *indexation*, which has been extensively reviewed in an excellent book by Herbert Giersch and others.[2] Indexation means the linking of financial agreements—mortgages, wages, taxes and others—to the rate of inflation. That is, these contracts are set in *real* terms, not nominal terms, through the use of what are commonly called "escalator" clauses. Such indexation can help reduce the side effects that must follow from ending inflation and reduce anticipations of future inflation.

The U.S. government already has escalator clauses on social security and other retirement benefits, the wages of many government employees, and other items. Taxes which are expressed as a certain percentage of price are also escalated automatically. Other escalator clauses are needed, however, if inflationary pressures are to be reduced to any extent.

The personal income tax could be easily adjusted so that rates were tied to the cost of living and the personal exemption and other deductions were raised according to inflation. These measures were adopted in Canada. In addition, the base for calculating capital gains can be adjusted to cover inflation, as can the base for calculating depreciation. For corporate taxation, these latter items could be included, as could book profits and losses.

Government securities could also be indexed, interest being paid in terms of the rise in the cost of living, rather than by a flat percentage. Such indexed bonds might prove so attractive under an inflationary situation that private enterprises would be forced to do the same. Because capital markets would begin to work in real terms, increased certainty and predictability in investment would result.

There is one major objection to the concept of indexation, which is in fact a misunderstanding of the principle, but which should be treated here. It is alleged that escalators actually have an inflationary effect on the economy, that the government has to expand the money supply to cover cost-of-living agreements as they respond to previous inflations. It should be noted, however, that escalators have *no* effect on the rate of inflation. They may allow an existing inflation to be transmitted more quickly and evenly through the economy (and this evenness might itself be an advantage in countering inflation) but this does not, in itself, raise or lower the rate of inflation. Adjustments for cost-of-living agreements come out of an existing expansion and do not prompt a future one.

OTHER WAYS TO FIGHT INFLATION

Other structural changes in the economy could help to reduce the pressure on governments to cause and prolong an inflationary over-stimulation. Some of these suggestions have been incorporated in an extensive anti-inflation package devised by Washington's Republican Study Committee,[3] and although these policies apply specifically to the United States, many of their lessons would be appropriate in other countries.

The first step would be to remove not only wage and price controls, but all other price manipulations by the government, and the power of government authorities to regulate prices and competition. Suitable targets for repeal are the "resale price maintenance" or state "fair trade" laws which exist in many countries and regions. Under these laws, all retailers are prevented from lowering their prices below a certain level; inefficiency and wastefulness are protected. This is, however, a luxury which we cannot afford if we are to come to grips with inflation.

A fresh look should be taken at the regulatory agencies, particularly the Civil Aeronautics Board, that has the power to keep air fares artificially high and to limit competition. A similar effect results from a country's membership in the International Air Transport Association, which fixes higher fares and lower standards of service than many of the airlines would wish to provide. In many countries, foreign and domestic air travel is a significant part of business costs; keeping air travel expensive keeps business costs—and therefore prices—artificially high.

Some federal safety regulations are far from cost-effective and constitute a new tax on businesses and individuals. Stringent safety standards in the automobile industry, for example, have served to increase prices and prevent competition and innovation—particularly in the development of small cars, where the cost of the safety standards is a large part of the overall cost of the vehicle. These costs could be cut by making some of the more stringent and expensive regulations optional. Then, those vehicle buyers who thought that the changes were really worth the cost could be satisfied. Similarly, the Occupational Safety and Health Act constitutes a "tax" on businesses. Often the costs are very large, especially for the small businessman, and the benefits minimal. Frequently, small businesses cannot afford to replace outmoded plants and machinery. That is why in the years following the implementation of OSHA, there has been a tendency to increased prices and simultaneously an increase in bankruptcies and unemployment.

Government monopoly in some services, such as the post office, is a statutory elimination of free competition. As such, the post office can charge whatever prices it likes and can offer standards of service that are much lower than those possible under competition. At present, the U.S. Postal Service makes use of United Parcel Service to deliver some of the parcel post. Furthermore, UPS can guarantee delivery within a specified period, which is more than the U.S. Postal

134

Service can do. The high cost of first class mail has caused some firms, such as certain electricity suppliers, to deliver bills by hand rather than through the mail. It has now become economical to invest large sums in major capital equipment so that accounts can in future be settled by telephone. Government monopolies such as the U.S. Postal Service are a luxury which the inflationary economy can well do without.

There are numerous other regulations designed to "protect" American farmers and industrialists, which in fact serve to keep prices high. Examples are the Meat Import Act, Dairy Import Quotas, the Jones Act (U.S. monopoly in coastal waters) and many more quota or price-support schemes.

MINIMUM WAGE LAWS

Minimum wage laws are also designed to "protect" workers, but in fact such inflationary laws raise prices and reduce employment.

Dr. Walter E. Williams, an economist at Temple University (and a Distinguished Scholar at The Heritage Foundation) has explained with eloquence the negative effect of minimum wage laws (another form of "price-fixing") on the employment of youth, especially minority youth. It is largely because of this government attempt at wage-fixing that upwards of half of minority teen-agers who are seeking work are unemployed in many of our large cities.

Writing in *Policy Review* (Fall 1977) Dr. Williams analyzed exactly how minimum wage laws reduce employment and add to inflation (further reducing employment).

> Federal and State minimum wage laws are acts of governmental intervention in the labor market that are intended to produce a pattern of events other than that produced in a free market. In practice, legislated minima specify a legal minimum hourly wage that can be paid. The legislated minima raise the wage to a level higher than that which would have occurred with free market forces.
>
> Legislative bodies have the power to legislate a wage increase, but unfortunately, they have not found a way to legislate a worker productivity increase. Further, while Congress can legislate the price of a labor transaction, it cannot require that the transaction actually be made. To the extent that the minimum wage law raises the pay level to that which may exceed the productivity of some workers, employers will predictably make adjustments in their use of labor. Such an adjustment will produce gains for some workers at the expense of other workers. Those workers who retain their jobs and receive a higher wage clearly gain. The adverse effects are borne by those workers who are most disadvantaged in terms of marketable skills, who lose their jobs and their income or who are not hired in the first place.
>
> This effect is more clearly seen if we put ourselves in the place of an employer and ask: If a wage of $2.60 per hour must be paid no matter who is hired, what kind of worker does it pay to hire?

135

Clearly the answer, in terms of economic efficiency, is to hire workers whose productivity is the closest to $2.60 per hour. If such workers are available, it clearly does not pay the firm to hire those workers whose output is say, $1.50 per hour. Even if the employer were willing to train such a worker, the fact that the worker must be paid a wage higher than the market value of his output plus the training cost makes on-the-job training an unattractive proposition.

The impact of legislated minima can be brought into sharper focus if we ask the distributional question: Who bears the burden of the minimum wage? As suggested earlier, the workers who bear the heaviest burden are those that are the most marginal. These are workers whom employers perceive as being less productive or more costly to employ than other workers. In the U.S. labor force, there are at least two segments of the labor force that share the marginal worker characteristics to a greater extent than do other segments of the labor force. The first group consists of youths in general. They are low-skilled or marginal because of their age, immaturity and lack of work experience. The second group, which contains members of the first group, are racial minorities such as Negroes and Hispanics, who as a result of racial discrimination and a number of other socioeconomic factors, are disproportionately represented among low-skilled workers. These workers are not only made unemployable by the minimum wage, but their opportunities to upgrade their skills through on-the-job training are also severely limited. [4]

THE ROOT CAUSE AND THE LASTING CURE

David I. Meiselman, the author of the foreword to this book, is a leading specialist in monetary economics. He has summed up the root cause of inflation and the only way it can be permanently ended in the following paragraphs.

Inflation is the most thoroughly researched topic in all of economics. Every inflation, including all contemporary inflations, has the same explanation. There are no exceptions to the rule.

The rule is that prices, on average, depend on the ratio of money to output.

Inflation results, as in recent years, when the quantity of money increases faster than output, the nation's total production of goods and services ("real" Gross National Product). Prices, on average, tend to be stable, as in much of the 1920s, when money increases at the same pace as output. There is deflation, prices fall, when, as in the thirty years after the end of the Civil War, money increases less than output.

Money, which consists of both cash (bills and coins) and bank deposits (checkbook and passbook money), is closely controlled by the Federal Reserve, our central bank and an agency of the federal government.

In the 1960s, when output increased an average of 6.6% per year, the

Federal Reserve increased the quantity of money by an average of 10.6% per year, or 4.0% per year faster than output. Consistent with the rule, inflation also averaged 4.0% per year.

Thus far in the 1970s, U.S. output has increased at the average rate of 2.1% per year. Because the Federal Reserve has increased money by 9.5% per year, or 7.4% faster than output, inflation has also averaged 7.4%. The old laws of economics still hold.

There is no way inflation can be slowed or eliminated unless the Federal Reserve also slows the growth of money to match the real growth of the economy.

It is the Federal Reserve rather than the coffee in Brazil, the freeze in Florida or even the Arab oil cartel which is the principal factor in the U.S. inflation story. Like so many other problems, inflation is largely made in Washington, not on Main Street or even Wall Street.[5]

If David Meiselman's advice is ultimately adopted by those who make economic policy in the United States, there will be no need for wage and price controls since inflation will be eliminated for all practical purposes.

FOOTNOTES

1. Phillip Cagan, *The Hydra-Headed Monster* (Washington, D.C.: American Enterprise Institute, 1974) p. 55.

2. Herbert Gierch, *et. al., Essays and Inflation and Indexation* (Washington, D.C.: American Enterprise Institute, 1974).

3. Republican Study Committee, U.S. House of Representatives, *50 ways to Fight Inflation* (Washington, D.C., 1975).

4. Walter E. Williams, "Government Sanctioned Restraints That Reduce Economic Opportunities For Minorities," *Policy Review* (Washington, D.C.: The Heritage Foundation) Fall 1977, reprinted [with revisions] July 1978, pp. 4–6.

In his article, Dr. Williams has cited other research which tends to substantiate his thesis. On p. 6 he refers the reader to the following works. David E. Kaun, "Minimum Wages, Factor Substitution, and the Marginal Producer," *Quarterly Journal of Economics,* August 1965, pp. 478–486; Yale Brozen, "The Effect of Statutory Minimum Wages on Teenage Unemployment," *Journal of Law and Economics,* April 1969, pp. 109–122; Marvin Kosters and Finis Welch, "The Effects of Minimum Wages on the Distribution of Changes in Aggregate Employment," *American Economic Review,* June 1972, pp. 323–332; William G. Bowen and T. Aldrich Finegan, *The Economics of Labor Force Participation* (Princeton University Press, 1969); Edmund S. Phelps, *Inflationary Policy and Unemployment Theory* (New York: W. W. Norton and Company, 1972); Arthur F. Burns, *The Management of Prosperity* (New York: Columbia University Press, 1966); Thomas G. Moore, "The Effect of Minimum Wages on Teenage Unemployment Rates," *Journal of Political Economy,* July/August 1971, pp. 897–902; James F. Ragan, Jr., "Minimum Wages and the Youth Labor Market," *The Review of Economics and Statistics,* May 1977, pp. 129–136; Martin Feldstein, "The Economics of the New Unemployment," *The Public Interest,* Fall 1973; Andrew Brimmer, *Minimum Wage Proposals, Labor Costs, and Employment Opportunities in the Nation's Capital* (Brimmer & Company, Inc., 1978) demonstrates the adverse employment and business migration effects of the minimum wage law in Washington, D.C.

5. David I. Meiselman, "Inflation, Who Did It?", National Public Policy Syndicate, New York, August 12, 1977.

19

The Economic Effects Of
Wage and Price Controls

Perhaps we can be thankful that wage and price controls can rarely be maintained over any long period, for there is a great deal of evidence that these controls, to the extent that they are successful, can cause severe and sometimes permanent damage to the economy. One of the most penetrating and effective accounts of these adverse effects of controls comes from C. Jackson Grayson, Jr., who was Chairman of the Price Commission under Phase II of the Nixon Economic Stabilization Policy. His attacks on price and wage manipulation began with *Confessions of a Price Controller*[1] and a magazine article of 1974 in which he remarks with graceful brevity that "as a result of my sixteen months as a price controller, I can list seven ways that controls interfere (negatively) with the market system and hasten its metamorphosis into a centralized economy."[2]

Let us briefly examine Grayson's seven points and add some comment to them:

(1) *Controls lead to distortions in the market system.* Hayek calls the free price system a "miracle" because it informs buyers and sellers of the relative scarcities of all products and simultaneously encourages them to restore supply and demand to equilibrium. For normal products, when demand exceeds supply, prices will be bid up. The prospect of higher profit margins will draw more sellers into the market or will encourage present sellers to increase their supply and hence supply and demand will once more be restored to equilibrium. When supply exceeds demand, prices will fall and buyers will absorb more of the product, while sellers will reduce their output. Equilibrium is once more restored.

When prices are manipulated, however, these "signals" indicating relative scarcity cannot be detected. It becomes impossible to distinguish real signals from artificial, manipulated ones. Shortages become common because firms are not induced by higher profitability to expand their supply. Black markets emerge to meet the demands of customers who would otherwise have to suffer long delays on the delivery of commodities at the controlled price. Firms that would be fully profitable under a freely-adjusting price mechanism are squeezed out of production or are not induced to enter production under artificially depressed prices.

In capital markets, these conditions create a major problem for investors; it becomes impossible to invest rationally when some firms are being driven to bankruptcy by the controls, when shortages are common but cannot be detected in terms of a price rise, and when black market operations account for a sizeable proportion of the trade of an industry. Consequently, the flow of investment funds to the various producing sectors in the economy becomes distorted, firms which would not be profitable under normal conditions are able to survive, and nothing is done to prevent the serious shortages that emerge through the imposition of controls.

This, of course, offers a good argument to those who would advocate the institution of a centralized economy. They say that the "market" is clearly unable to allocate resources properly, and to keep supply and demand in equilibrium. Controls themselves make further government intervention (to correct the disequilibria caused by controls) more likely.

(2) *Controls penalize those who wish to claim non-inflationary wage or price increases.* "During a period of controls," says Grayson, "the public forgets that not all wage-price increases are inflationary." A wage increase, for example, is not inflationary if it does not lead to the government borrowing or increasing credit and money supply to satisfy it. If some particular firm has a good performance record, and is enjoying a larger share of the market and higher profits, it is natural that it might wish to pass on some of these higher profits to its labor force. This increase would not be inflationary, since it comes out of profits that are willingly given to the firm by consumers. Wage controls, however, would stop this transfer of profits from firms to workers, since they never distinguish between inflationary and non-inflationary wage increases.

(3) *Controls negate the profit principle.* Controls are introduced when the government declares that prices, or the rise in prices, are "too high." This suggests that there is something that sellers can do about their prices, if only they were public-spirited or if they were forced. It further suggests that profits are also "too high," but it is through the profit motive that investment resources are drawn to worthwhile industries and so, by calling this motive into question, controls undermine the philosophy of the free market and cause dislocations in capital formation and investment.

(4) *Controls can be used for noneconomic motives.* The fourth instance in which price controls may damage the economy is when lobbyists ask for them in order to fulfill noneconomic objectives. There are controls on the price of food, for example, they say, because food is important to consumers. If this is true, then why not have controls on the prices of firms which cause pollution, or do not employ sufficient numbers of minorities? This is the beginning of the political manipulation of the market system.

(5) *Controls engender comfortable attitudes.* Grayson says that "wage-price controls can easily become a security blanket against the cold winds of free-market uncertainties." In the market, decisions have to be made, profits rise or fall, firms succeed or go bankrupt, and men are given jobs or laid off. Under control, the illusion is sometimes maintained, at least in the short term, that

140

these decisions do not have to be faced. The behavior of prices and wages is predictable under controls and, therefore, they do not have to be taken into consideration in the decisions of firms.

(6) *The regulatory body becomes more important than the market.* Under controls, business and labor leaders begin to pay more attention to the mechanism of regulation than to the dynamics of the marketplace. Years of wage regulation in Britain, for example, have encouraged a situation in which the trade union leaders are, in effect, another branch of government and are consulted by government officials before any economic policy can be put into effect.

Employers and union leaders themselves, observing that wages and prices can be fixed or increased only by the agreement of some regulatory body, pay more attention to influencing the decisions of that body in their own favor than they do to improving their market performance and the productivity of their labor.

(7) *Controls draw attention away from the real causes of inflation.* Grayson says that price controls "draw attention away from the fundamental factors that affect inflation—fiscal and monetary policies, tax rates, import-export policies, productivity, competitive restrictions, and the like."[3] There is an enduring belief that controls are a cure for inflation itself, not merely temporary suspensions of its symptoms.

OTHER ECONOMIC EFFECTS

There are some other comments on the economic effects of wage and price controls that might be given here:

Firstly, as Roger Blough writes in the *Monthly Labor Review*, "Controls sometimes . . . do a disservice by masking the need for structural reforms where needed in the economy."[4] It is not merely that controls draw attention away from the real causes of inflation, but that they give governments an excuse for inaction. "Controls put a damper on inflation without seeming to require restraints on aggregate demand or any increase in unemployment," remarks Phillip Cagan.[5] Small wonder that they are so popular with politicians!

Secondly, controls shift the traditional economic powers wielded by government, labor organizations, businesses and consumers. For the most part, power is put into the hands of the former three at the expense of the latter. Once more, this process has reached a critical stage in Britain, where price controls have been in effect over long periods since World War II. *The Free Nation* remarks caustically that "Incomes policies arouse the bargaining powers of the unions," giving them a rallying-point from which further support can be drummed up, and "can lead to unjustifiable union arrogance. . . . Detailed concern by the government in wage negotiations ascribes more influence to the trade unions than economic experience shows is their due. Voluntary incomes policies which solicit the blessing of union leaders . . . make the unions appear as allies of

141

stability and responsibility instead of their principal enemy."[6] Like the unions, the government, by taking upon itself the important economic task of setting wages and prices, of intervening in wage disputes and other crucial activities, expands its economic influence to gigantic proportions when compared to its influence in a free economy.

A minor but interesting effect of recent British and American wage and price restrictions has been the introduction of "list prices." If a retailer believes that his prices are going to be frozen by the government, he will tend to fix an artificially high list price and then offer his goods at a considerable discount on that price. By this means, the retailer maintains a degree of slackness that can absorb the effects of the controls. Hence, in those two countries and others, scores of "discount shops" have sprung up, particularly in the luxury goods sectors, where the range of controls is wide. So, in this situation, the real (selling) price continues to rise as sellers' costs rise, while the cosmetic (list) price remains static, fixed by the controls. Were it possible to calculate the impact of this effect upon real and reported inflation, then the notion that controls really are able to hold down selling prices would receive yet another blow and the Consumer Price Index would edge higher than it has been doing during the recent inflations in the Western world.

There are two more ways, in addition to Grayson's seven considerations, in which wage and price controls serve to dislocate the price system and disrupt production. Controls, it will be noted, are always imposed during a period of inflation, when prices are rising and workers are claiming higher wages to keep abreast of the increased cost of living and are struggling to retain their wage differentials with other groups of workers. Similarly, sellers are raising their prices to pass on these cost increases without reducing profit margins. In this situation, as Phillip Cagan notes,[7] "There is never any right moment when an inflationary process can be frozen by decree without imposing hardships on many sellers who need to raise prices to cover recent cost increases." Similarly, hardships are imposed on workers who find themselves behind in the struggle to maintain traditional differentials. In addition to dislocating prices and wages, therefore, controls serve to promote unrest among workers and sellers alike.

The second instance in which controls disrupt the economy takes place not when they are imposed, but when they are lifted. "Controls are unlikely even to make the ultimate total rise in prices less than it would have been had they not been imposed, given the same path of aggregate demand," writes Cagan.[8] "Prices gravitate toward an equilibrium determined by the interaction of demand and supply conditions. Constraints such as controls can delay the adjustment, but eventually prices will find their equilibrium. . . after the controls are lifted."

There is one last economic effect of wage and price controls that might be mentioned here. The common rationale for controls is that they curb the bargaining power of the large unions and reduce the ability of the large corporations to force prices up. As we have seen, their effect is quite the opposite with respect to the power of the unions and with respect to the power of the large corporations; the evidence suggests that these firms do not initiate inflationary increases, but usually fall behind in the inflationary process. Large firms incur higher administrative costs in making a price change, there is a reluctance among oligopolists to start price wars, and a large firm is unable to be sure of what the "equilibrium" price really is for a wide-selling range of products. Consequently, there is a reluctance among large firms to change their prices when an inflationary movement begins. Controls serve only to keep them further behind, so there is no economic reason that the great weight of the controls should be directed at the large corporations.

CONTROLS AND EMPLOYMENT

Controls may increase employment in two ways. The first and most important is that they reduce anticipations of price increases. In the unregulated inflationary economy, there is always a tendency for wage claims and price rises to result in overestimated predictions of future price rises. Often it is impossible even to guess just what future price rises will be, so workers and sellers tend to set their price and wage claims at the higher end of the range of possibilities. This insulates them from future, anticipated price rises. Prices and wages are set far above their equilibrium price, and an inflationary pressure is the consequence. If controls reduce anticipated price rises, then prices can be brought into line with the equilibria, and the inflationary pressure is reduced. "The fact of the controls. . . ," reported the Council of Economic Advisers in 1974,[9] "reduced inflationary expectations, held down total spending, restrained the tendency to boost wages and prices, and permitted output to rise more rapidly than it would otherwise have done."

A second way in which controls seem to increase employment can be seen in the formation of public service regulatory bodies to administer the controls themselves! The number of agencies that have been created for price regulation is staggering. Consider: The *National Board for Prices and Incomes*; the *Council on Prices, Productivity and Incomes*; the *National Economic Development Council*; the *National Incomes Commission*. So far, these organizations are the only ones in Britain. We must not forget the Dutch *Board of Government Mediators*, the *Social and Economic Council*, and the *Central Planning Board*. In France there were the *Conference des Revenus*, the *National Accounting Commission* and the *Center for the Study of Incomes and Costs*.

Wage controls were a major part of the work of the German *Council of Economic Experts* and of the Austrian *Federal Chamber of Industry and Trade*, as well as the latter country's *Economic Commission*. The Austrian *Joint Commission for Prices and Wages* examined the subject of controls full time, as did the *Advisory Council for Economic and Social Questions*. The Danish *Economic Council* was another such agency with the primary purpose of administering

143

controls; and, moving across oceans, there are the Canadian *Economic Council*, the *Prices and Incomes Commission*, as well as the United States *Price Commission*, and various subcommittees of the *Council of Economic Advisors*.

Wage and price controls, it seems, require such a multitude of agencies, commissions, councils and boards to administer them. Each organization has its own research and economic experts, executives, planners, members, and supervisors. The employment potential of the administration of price controls (although quite unproductive) is apparently enormous!

In the private sector, however, controls undoubtedly increase unemployment, although the employment function is so complicated that no hard and fast quantitative answer can be given to the question of the precise effect of controls on employment. From a common sense position, however, we can agree with the British economist Sam Brittan, who says,[10] "A price ceiling that squeezes profits in relation to wages is, from the employer's point of view, equivalent to an increase in real wages. It thus becomes less profitable to employ as many people as before." As margins are squeezed, of course, it is the less-valued workers who will be the first to go, but the marginal workforce is made up of exactly those people—poorer paid and less skilled workers—whom price controls are designed to help. It was because of this unemployment effect as much as any other that the Labor government in Sam Brittan's own country ended price controls when they acceded to power in 1974 and gave some industries tax relief in order to rescue their eroding margins.

Brittan cites a subtle effect of price controls that might be recounted here. The same unemployment effect can occur, he says, when controls are removed, as happened in the United Kingdom in the winter of 1971:[11]

> Faced with a sudden acceleration of money wage increases following the abandonment of incomes control, employers became less confident about passing them on in higher prices—partly because the effect of [the then Chancellor of the Exchequer] Roy Jenkins's monetary restraint was still being felt, but also because they were unsure how their competitors would react to an unprecedented situation. The result was an increase in the share of wages relative to profits, above what was normal in the downward phase of the [business] cycle, and a level of unemployment in the winter of 1971–2 that surprised the official forecasters.

Such an effect cannot be permanent, of course, as firms eventually discover how much they can raise prices following the abandonment of controls, without initiating price warfare from other firms. Nevertheless, the effect is disrupting to business and is harmful for the employment prospects of the workforce.

Moreover, the phenomenon strikes publicly-owned industries as well as private ones. A price ceiling coupled with continually rising costs will reduce the profit margins (or more likely, will increase the deficits) of public industries. These losses have to be financed out of taxation, or through government borrowing, which is a further pressure on the inflation rate.

Sir John Hicks once warned that "When the real demand for labor falls (as it has fallen) then traditional theory says that either there must be a fall in real wages or there must be unemployment."[12] Under price restraint, the demand for labor certainly does fall as margins are squeezed. The ingenious government of Great Britain found a way out of such a dilemma between falling wages and unemployment by preventing employers from declaring their workers jobless. The effect which this featherbedding has had on the British economy is now only too well known: firms have been unable to survive under the constricting regulations, the number of bankruptcies has risen dramatically, and both capital and initiative have been drained out of the country.

FOOTNOTES

1. C. Jackson Grayson, Jr., *Confessions of a Price Controller* (New York: Dow-Jones, Irwin, 1974).

2. C. Jackson Grayson, Jr., "Controls are Not the Answer," *Challenge*, November-December 1974, p. 10.

3. *Ibid.*, p. 12.

4. Roger M. Blough, "Minimizing the Effect of Controls," *Monthly Labor Review*, Vol. 97, No. 3, March 1974.

5. Phillip Cagan, *The Hydra-Headed Monster* (Washington, D.C.: American Enterprise Institute, 1974) p. 55.

6. "The Fatal Temptation," *The Free Nation* (London: National Association for Freedom) September 3, 1976, p. 9.

7. Phillip Cagan, *The Hydra-Headed Monster* (Washington, D.C.: American Enterprise Institute, 1974) p. 55.

8. *Ibid.*, p. 56.

9. *Annual Report of the Council of Economic Advisors*, February 1974, p. 99.

10. Samuel Brittan, *Second Thoughts on Full Employment Policy* (London: Barry Rose, for the Centre for Policy Studies, 1975) p. 48.

11. *Ibid.*, p. 50.

12. Sir John Hicks, *Crisis '75. . .?* (London: Institute of Economic Affairs, 1975). See especially pp. 17–25.

20

Summary and Conclusion

The record of governmental attempts to control wages and prices is clear. Such efforts have been made in one form or another periodically in almost all times and all places since the very beginning of organized society. In all times and in all places they have just as invariably failed to achieve their announced purposes. Time after time an historian has laconically concluded, ". . . the plan to control rising prices failed utterly." Or, ". . . the laws were soon repealed since no one paid any attention to them."

In Egypt, government controls over the grain crop led gradually to ownership of all the land by the state. In Babylon, in Sumeria, in China, in India, in Greece and in Rome various kinds of regulations over the economy were tried and usually either failed completely or produced harmful effects. One of the most well-known cases of wage and price controls in the ancient world occurred in the time of the Emperor Diocletian. Thousands of people throughout the Empire were put to death before these futile laws were finally repealed.

In the Middle Ages, the city of Antwerp fell to the Spanish largely because no one would risk bringing food to the besieged city if he could not obtain the market price once he had passed by the Spanish guns.

In the American colonies, frequent attempts were made to keep down the price of beaverskins and suchlike commodities. All failed. Indians as well as the European colonists insisted on market prices for their goods and labor.

During the American War of Independence, Washington's army nearly starved at Valley Forge largely due to what John Adams called "That improvident Act for limiting prices [which] has done great injury, and [which] in my sincere opinion, if not repealed will ruin the state and introduce a civil war."[1] As one economic historian explained, "The regulation of prices by law had precisely the opposite effect to that intended; for prices were increased rather than diminished by the adoption of the measure."[2] The same historian concluded that "Tried by facts, the measure was a total failure in achieving the end proposed by its authors and ultimately had not a defender."[3]

With the coming of the Revolution in France, successive governments still failed to learn from experience. A series of so-called "Maximum Price" laws were passed and all proved ineffectual. We are told that in Paris of 1794 one observer reported that "one hundred and fifty women had crowded up to a butcher's door at four o'clock in the morning. They screamed out that it was better to pay twenty or thirty sous and have what they wanted than to pay fourteen, the maximum price, and get nothing."[4]

With the advent of the nineteenth century the Western world was blessed by a happy period of relative peace and prosperity. For 100 years no major wars were fought by the European powers and the principles of free trade reached their ascendancy. Shortly after Victoria came to the British throne, the famous Corn Laws (which for generations kept the price of bread higher than market levels) were repealed. As we have seen, the British authorities in India managed to avert a disastrous famine in 1866 by allowing the prices of food to fluctuate with the market, thus insuring a speedy and equitable distribution of rice and grain where they were needed most.

CONTROLS IN TWO WORLD WARS

With the breakdown of the structure of peace in 1914, however, both the Allies and the Central Powers insisted on returning to the drawing board with entirely predictable results. Even in the Organized State *par excellence* (the Kaiser's Germany), economists pronounced price and wage controls to be ineffective. No other nation, democracy or dictatorship, monarchy or republic, managed to make them work.

During the Second World War and shortly thereafter, price and wage controls once again were resorted to by the major nations. Although a supreme patriotic effort in several nations (including the United States) slowed the *official* rise in wages and prices a bit, it is probable that the *real* prices and wages were affected little. Besides encouraging a thriving black market, wage and price controls resulted in a reduction in quality of goods and increased "perquisites" for jobs (fringe benefits, overtime, and so on), all contributing to a double system: the "official," controlled prices and wages and the "unofficial" real prices and wages.

In both the United States and Britain in the 1970s, two governments which were elected by conservatives imposed wage and price controls with essentially the same results. The various "Phases" of President Nixon were completely ineffectual in controlling inflation (in fact, there is some evidence that inflation was actually worsened by the controls themselves, to say nothing of other government policies). The "Stages" of Prime Minister Edward Heath met the same fate except that in Britain, due largely to the Conservative government's complete lack of monetary restraint, the inflation rate passed 25 percent. Not to be outdone, in 1975, Prime Minister Pierre Trudeau of Canada invoked a similar program for his own nation. The labor unions replied with a general strike and opposition from all economic classes and political philosophies has been very vocal. Canadian controls were ended in April 1978.

PRESIDENT CARTER'S VOLUNTARY CONTROLS

With the election of Jimmy Carter as President of the United States, the former Georgia Governor immediately began receiving advice from many quarters (fortunately by no means all) that wage and price controls might be necessary in the near future. Mr. Hobart Rowen, for instance, in his economic column for *The Washington Post* (December 12, 1976, p. M1) began by admitting that

> It is of course true that organized labor, as represented by AFL-CIO president George Meany, has vigorously opposed wage-price controls and explicit wage-price guidelines.
>
> But the preponderance of the advice Carter is getting focuses on the need to expand the U.S. economy and reduce unemployment. These efforts involve the risk of a new inflation—if not right away, then when activity moves closer to the economy's capacity.
>
> To make both goals—greater employment and control of inflation—compatible, fiscal and monetary policy must be supplemented by voluntary wage-price restraints—sometimes called "incomes policies."
>
> The United States is the only major industrial nation without an incomes policy.

Ralph Nader, in a recent column (*The Washington Star*, June 17, 1978), warned that ". . . should inflation remain at current or higher levels, Carter will find it difficult to avoid imposing a selective, mandatory price-wage control policy in . . . key industries."

And, of course, the talented novelist from Cambridge, Massachusetts, John Kenneth Galbraith (who has never been happier than when he was serving his country in the Office of Price Administration) chimes in periodically with the same advice.

Even the defenders of wage and price controls recognize that they result in distortions in the use of economic resources, add heavy extra costs and at least *may* still fail to reduce inflation.

When President Carter announced his new program of voluntary wage and price guidelines on October 24, 1978, he was careful to say that he still opposed mandatory controls and did not intend to ask Congress for the authority to impose them. The AFL-CIO, however, almost immediately endorsed mandatory controls as preferable to voluntary controls. As this book went to press in late 1978, many were predicting mandatory controls in one form or another in 1979.

Most economists would agree that controls produce uncertainty and hesitation. Many businessmen hold back and fail to expand into new areas and add new employees because they are not sure what will be the latest government regulation. Controls also cost millions of man-hours in both government and industry; the great expense of administering countless regulations (if we assume their effect is negligible or negative) must be recorded as colossal waste. As profits approach legal ceilings, businessmen have less reason to keep down costs; this also leads to waste of valuable resources. Insofar as wage controls actually hold down salaries, employees are not stimulated to do their work or to seek better jobs and employers are restrained from securing as many and as highly skilled workers as they could productively use.

Although many economists would concede that government controls are able to restrain prices for very short periods of time (by so-called "freezes"), the end result is that pent-up inflation bursts at the first opportunity, giving rise to even higher prices in the long run. This effect has been recognized at least since the very beginning of our Republic; John Adams wrote to his wife in 1777 that "I expect only a partial and temporary relief from [rising prices by means of controls] and I fear that after a time the evils will break out with greater violence. The matter will flow with greater rapidity for having been dammed up for a time."[5]

COMING FULL CIRCLE IN EGYPT

And in Egypt, where this book began twenty chapters ago, history (as it sometimes does) has come full circle. Price and wage controls as enforced by the current Egyptian government have resulted in unforeseen (and unwanted) consequences not unlike the effects of such policies pursued by their predecessors four thousand (and five thousand) years ago. Because the government (for "good" reasons) has tried to keep the price of bread below market levels, a good deal of the supply is being fed to animals, since it is cheaper than hay. The result, of course, is that many people in the cities are going hungry.[6]

In addition to the many economic difficulties which cannot be dismissed with such quips as Lord Keynes' dictum that "in the long run we are all dead," there remains an underlying moral problem. The government of the United States was scarcely a year old when a writer in *The Connecticut Courant* asserted that "the scheme of supporting the money and regulating the price of things by penal statutes . . . always has and ever will be impracticable in a free country, because no law can be framed to limit a man in the purchase or disposal of property, but what must infringe those principles of liberty for which we are gloriously fighting."[7]

As Milton Friedman pointed out in 1971 after President Nixon had imposed his version of wage and price controls:

> The controls are deeply and inherently immoral. By substituting the rule of men for the rule of law and for voluntary cooperation in the marketplace, the controls threaten the very foundations of a free society. By encouraging men to spy and report on one another, by making it in the private interest of large numbers of citizens to evade the controls, and by making actions illegal that are in the public interest, the controls undermine individual morality.[8]

If an historian were to sum up what we have learned from the long history of wage and price controls in this country and in many others around the world, he would have to conclude that the only thing we learn from history is that we do not learn from history.

150

As America's first well-known economist, Pelatiah Webster, observed when describing the effects of the unhappy experiment with economic controls during our War of Independence,

> It seemed to be a kind of obstinate delirium, totally deaf to every argument drawn from justice and right, from its natural tendency and mischief, from common sense and even from common safety[9] . . . . It is not more absurd to attempt to impel faith into the heart of an unbeliever by fire and fagot, or to whip love into your mistress with a cowskin, than to force value or credit into your money by penal laws.[10]

FOOTNOTES

1. Albert Bolles, *The Financial History of the United States* (New York, 1896) Vol. 1, pp. 165–66.

2. *Ibid.*, p. 166.

3. *Ibid.*, p. 173.

4. Henry Bourne, "Food Control and Price-Fixing in Revolutionary France," *The Journal of Political Economy*, March 1919, p. 208.

5. Bolles, *op. cit.*, p. 159.

6. *The Washington Post*, April 29, 1978, p. A16.

7. *The Connecticut Courant*, May 12, 1777.

8. Milton Friedman, *An Economist's Protest* (N.J.: Glen Ridge, 1975) p. 129.

9. Pelatiah Webster, *Political Essays* (Philadelphia, 1791) p. 129.

10. *Ibid.*, p. 132.

Appendix A

The Wage and Price Control Statutes From the Code of Hammurabi

The Code of Hammurabi was promulgated in Babylon approximately 4,000 years ago (the exact date is uncertain; the best estimate for the concluding year of the king's reign is 2150 B.C.). The text is from *The Hammurabi Code and the Sinaitic Legislation* by Chilperic Edwards (Kennikat Press, N.Y., 1904, pp. 67–73). Provisions which do not refer to price and wage controls have been omitted, hence the gaps in the numbering of the clauses.

239. If a man hire a boatman, he shall give him six *gur* of corn per annum.

242. If a man hires for a year, the fee for a draught ox is four *gur* of corn.

243. The fee for a milch-cow is three *gur* of corn given to the owner.

245. If a man has hired an ox, and by neglect or by blows has caused its death, he shall replace ox by ox to the owner of the ox.

257. If a man hire a field-labourer, he shall give him eight *gur* of corn per annum.

258. If a man hire a herdsman, he shall give him six *gur* of corn per annum.

261. If a man hire a pasturer for cattle and sheep, he shall give him eight *gur* of corn per annum.

268. If a man has hired an ox for threshing, twenty *qa* of corn is its hire.

269. If an ass has been hired for threshing, ten *qa* of corn is its hire.

270. If a young animal has been hired for threshing, one *qa* of corn is its hire.

271. If a man hire cattle, wagon, and driver, he shall give 180 *qa* of corn per diem.

272. If a man has hired a wagon by itself, he shall give forty *qa* of corn per diem.

273. If a man hire a workman, then from the beginning of the year until the fifth month he shall give six grains of silver per diem. From the sixth month until the end of the year he shall give five grains of silver per diem.

274. If a man hire a son of the people,

Pay of a potter	five grains of silver,
Pay of a tailor	five grains of silver,
Pay of a carpenter	four grains of silver,
Pay of a ropemaker	four grains of silver,

he shall give per diem.

275. If a man hire a *[illegible], her hire is three grains of silver per diem.

276. If a man hire a *makhirtu*, he shall give two and a half grains of silver per diem for her hire.

277. If a man hire a sixty-ton boat, he shall give a sixth part of a shekel of silver per diem for her hire.

. . .The judgments of justice which Hammurabi, the mighty king, has estab-

* Partially legible provisions have been omitted.

lished, conferring upon the land a sure guidance and a gracious rule.

Hammurabi, the protecting king, am I. I have not withdrawn myself from the blackheaded race that Bel has entrusted to me, and over whom Merodach has made me shepherd. I have not reposed myself upon my side; but I have given them places of peace. Difficult points have I made smooth, and radiance have I shed abroad. With the mighty weapon that Zamama and Ishtar have lent me; with the penetration with which Ea has endowed me; with the valour that Merodach has given me, I have rooted out all enemies above and below; and the depths have I subjugated. The flesh of the land I have made rejoice: the resident people I have made secure; I have not suffered them to be afraid. . . .

Appendix B

The Edict of Diocletian Fixing Maximum Prices and Wages

This remarkable document exists in no French or German and in only one almost complete English translation* which is presented here. The preamble is published almost in its entirety and a representative sample of the more than one thousand individual prices and wages is appended to it.

"1. The national honor and the dignity and majesty of Rome demand that the fortune of our State—to which, next to the immortal gods, we may, in memory of the wars which we have successfully waged, return thanks for the tranquil and profoundly quiet condition of the world—be also faithfully administered and duly endowed with the blessings of that peace for which we have laboriously striven; to the end that we, who under the gracious favor of the gods have repressed the furious depredations, in the past, of barbarous tribes by the destructions of those nations themselves, may for all time gird with the bulwarks due to justice the peace which has been established.

"2. To be sure, if any spirit of self-restraint were holding in check those practices by which the raging and boundless avarice is inflamed, an avarice which, without regard for the human race, not yearly or monthly or daily only, but almost every hour and even every moment, hastens toward its own development and increase; or if the common fortunes could with calmness bear this orgy of license, by which, under their unhappy star, they are from day to day ripped to pieces—peradventure there would seem to be room left for shutting our eyes and holding our peace, since the united endurance of men's minds would ameliorate this detestable enormity and pitiable condition.

"3. But since it is the sole desire of untamed fury to feel no love for the ties of our common humanity; and since among the wicked and lawless it is held to be, so to speak, the religious duty of an avarice that swells and grows with fierce flames, that, in harrying the fortunes of all, it should desist of necessity rather than voluntarily. . .

*The English text is taken from the distinguished essay entitled "The Edict of Diocletian Fixing Maximum Prices" by Roland G. Kent which was published in *The University of Pennsylvania Law Review* for 1920 (pp. 35–47). Professor Kent included an explanatory note giving credit for the joint authorship which is reproduced here. "In French and in German," he wrote, "there exist, apparently, no translations, but only some much-abridged summaries; in English there is a translation by Professor Rolfe, of the University of Pennsylvania, and Professor Tarbell, of the University of Chicago, presented with much hesitancy on their part, and running only to the middle of the eleventh sentence, where the Plataean fragment which they were editing comes to an end. In presenting herewith a complete translation of the preamble, therefore, the author is moved by the desirability of having it accessible to students in an English form, and he is not unaware of his own temerity in attempting the task; but he is reassured by the kindness of Professor Rolfe, who has consented to the use of his and Tarbell's translation, so far as it goes, with such verbal changes as the present writer cares to make."

155

"4. And of this matter, it is true, as the common knowledge of all recognizes and indisputable facts proclaim, the consideration is almost too late, since we form plans or delay discovered remedies in the hope that, as was to be expected from natural justice, humanity, detected in most odious crimes, might work out its own reformation; for we thought it far better that the censure of intolerable robbery should be removed from the court of public opinion by the feeling and decision of those men themselves, who rush daily from bad to worse and in a sort of blindness of mind tend toward outrages upon society, and whom their grave misdoing has branded as enemies alike to individuals and to the community, and guilty of the most atrocious inhumanity.

"5. Therefore we proceed promptly to apply the remedies long demanded by the necessity of the case, and that too, feeling no concern about complaints that our corrective interference may, as coming unseasonably or unnecessarily, be considered cheaper or less valuable even in the eyes of the wicked, who, though seeing in our silence of so many years a lesson in self-restraint, nevertheless refused to follow it.

"6. For who has so dull a breast, or is so alien to the feeling of humanity, that he can be ignorant, nay rather has not actually observed that in commodities which are bought and sold in markets or handled in the daily trade of cities, the wantonness in prices had progressed to such a point that the unbridled greed for plundering might be moderated neither by abundant supplies nor by fruitful seasons?

"7. So that there is clearly no doubt that men of this sort, whom these occupations have engaged, are always mentally calculating and even seeking, from the motions of the stars, to take advantage of the very winds and seasons, and by reason of their wickedness cannot bear that the fields be watered and made productive by the rains of heaven, so as to give hope of future crops, since they consider it a personal loss for abundance to come to the world by the favorable moods of the sky itself.

"8. And to the avarice of those who are always eager to turn to their own profit even the blessings of the gods, and to check the tide of general prosperity, and again in an unproductive year to haggle about the sowing of the seed and the business of retail dealers; who, individually possessed of immense fortunes which might have enriched whole peoples to their heart's content, seek private gain and are bent upon ruinous percentages of profit—to their avarice, ye men of our provinces, regard for common humanity impels us to set a limit.

"9. But now, further, we must set forth the reasons themselves, whose urgency has at last compelled us to discard our too long protracted patience, in order that—although an avarice which runs riot through the whole world can with difficulty be laid bare by a specific proof, or rather fact—none the less the nature of our remedy may be known to be more just, when utterly lawless men shall be forced to recognize, under a definite name and description, the unbridled lusts of their minds.

"10. Who therefore can be ignorant that an audacity that plots against the good of society is presenting itself with a spirit of profiteering, wherever the general welfare requires our armies to be directed, not only in villages and towns, but along every highway? That it forces up the prices of commodities not fourfold or eightfold, but to such a degree that human language cannot find words to set a proper evaluation upon their action? Finally, that sometimes by the outlay upon a single article the soldier is robbed both of his bounty and of his pay, and that the entire contributions of the whole world for maintaining the armies accrue to the detestable gains of plunderers, so that our soldiers seem to yield the entire fruit of their military career, and the labors of their entire term of service, to these profiteers in everything, in order that the pillagers of the commonwealth may from day to day carry off all that they resolve to have?

"11. Being justly and duly moved by all these considerations above included, since already humanity itself seemed to be praying for release, we resolved, not that the prices of commodities should be fixed—for it is not thought just that this be done, since sometimes very many provinces exult in the good fortune of the low prices which they desire, and as it were in a certain privileged state of abundance—but that a maximum be fixed; in order that, when any stress of high prices made its appearance—which omen we prayed the gods might avert— avarice, which could not be checked on the so-to-speak endlessly extending plains, might be confined by the bounds of our statute and the limits set in the law promulgated to control them.

"12. It is our pleasure, therefore, that those prices, which the concise items of the following list indicate, be held in attention throughout our whole domain, in such a way that all men understand that freedom to exceed them is removed; while at the same time, in those places where goods manifestly abound, the happy condition of cheap prices shall not thereby be hampered—and ample provision is made for cheapness, if avarice is limited and curbed.

"13. Between sellers, moreover, and buyers whose custom it is to enter trading-ports and visit provinces overseas, this restraint will have to be a mutual action, that, while they already of themselves know that in the need imposed by high prices the price-limits cannot be exceeded, at the time of retailing such a reckoning of places and bargainings and of the whole transaction be figured out, that under it there is manifestly a fair agreement that those who transport the goods shall nowhere sell at an unduly high price.

"14. Because, therefore, it is an established fact that among our ancestors also the methods employed in new enactments was that boldness be curbed by a prescribed penalty—since very rarely is a status found for men which will benefit them with their free consent, but it is always fear, justest teacher of duties, which will restrain and guide them in the right path—it is our pleasure that if anyone have acted with boldness against the letter of this statute, he shall be subjected to capital punishment.

"15. And let none think that a hard penalty is set, though when the time comes the observance of moderation will be a refuge for averting the peril.

"16. He also shall be subject to the same peril, who in eagerness to purchase has come to an agreement with an avarice which retails in violation of the statutes.

"17. From such guilt also he too shall not be considered free, who, having goods necessary for food or usage, shall after this regulation have thought that they might be withdrawn from the market; since the penalty ought to be even heavier for him who causes need than for him who makes use of it contrary to the statutes.

"18. We therefore appeal to the devotion of all, that the decision made for the public welfare be observed with generous obedience and due scrupulousness, especially since by such a statute provision is manifestly made not only for the individual states and peoples and provinces, but for the whole world, for whose ruin a few, we learn, have raged exceedingly, whose greed neither length of time nor the riches which they are seen to have desired, have been able to moderate or satisfy."

Roland Kent notes (p. 45):

> After the preamble come the price lists arranged in schedules. The prices are fixed in the denarius, no longer a silver coin but one of copper, the value of which at the time of Diocletian was established by the discovery of a fragment of the Edict, in which the price of one Roman pound of refined gold was set at 50,000 denarii; the copper denarius was therefore worth .434 cents. Many of the items in the schedules are for commodities no longer current, and others are preserved in so fragmentary a state that the prices cannot be read. A few of the more interesting items of the various schedules are given below, with the weights, measures and prices changed into United States standards of the present day. [1920] [1]

Barley	per bushel	$	.873
Rye, or Oats[2]	per bushel		.524
Dried beans	per quart		.054
Old wine	per quart		.181
Beer	per quart		.03
Olive oil, best quality	per quart		.30
Vinegar	per quart		.045
Salt	per bushel		.873
Pork	per pound		.072
Beef	per pound		.048
Best Bacon	per pound		.096
Best Ham	per pound		.117
Male Pheasant, fatted	each		1.085
Hens	pair		.2604

Hare	each	.651
Peacock	each	1.302
Quail	each	.0868
Lamb	per pound	.0718
Sea fish	per pound	.145
Partridges	each	.1302
River fish	per pound	.072
Oysters	per hundred	.435
Artichokes	per five	.0434
Lettuce	per head	.0174
Onions, fresh	per twenty-five	.0174
Cultivated asparagus	per twenty-five	.026
Eggs	per dozen	.0521
Apples, best	per ten	.0174
Sheep's milk	per quart	.06
Fresh cheese	per quart	.07
Farm laborers[3]	per day	.108
Mason, carpenter	per day	.217
Wall decorator	per day	.651
Baker	per day	.217
Ship worker	per day	.26
Barber	per man	.087
Teacher of reading and writing	per pupil monthly	.217
Teacher of Greek and Latin	per pupil monthly	.808
Teacher of public speaking	per pupil monthly	1.08
Lawyer, for getting the matter before a court	per case	1.08
Lawyer, for services during trial	per case	4.34
Ox hide, tanned		3.255
Beaver's skin, tanned		.13
Leopard's skin, tanned		5.425
Seal skin, tanned		6.51
Country worker's shoes		.521
Patrician's shoes		.651
Woman's shoes		.26
Fir or Pine beams, 2000 board feet		217.00
Transportation, one person, one mile		.0094
Wagon load of 866 lbs.	per mile	.0945
Camel load of 433 lbs.	per mile	.0378
Raw silk	per pound	72.18
Washed Wool, fine	per pound	1.052
Washed Wool, ordinary	per pound	.15

FOOTNOTES

1. Weights were measured in the *pondo* or *libra*, the pound, which was equal to .722 lbs. avoirdupois and to .875 lbs. troy; and in the *uncia*, the ounce, which was one-twelfth of the Roman pound, or .963 oz. avoirdupois and .875 oz. troy.

   Lengths were measured by the *cubitus*, the ell, or 17.46 inches; and by the *digitus*, the finger, one twenty-fourth of the ell, or .73 inches.

   Dry commodities sold in bulk were measured by the *Italicus modius*, the Italian peck, which equaled 7.95 dry quarts, or almost precisely one peck; the *castrensis modius*, the military peck, had double the capacity of the Italian peck. The *Italicus sextarius*, the Italian pint, was one-sixteenth of the *Italicus modius*, and was therefore a trifling decimal under one dry pint; it was, however, employed mainly for liquids and equaled .578 liquid quarts.

   Other goods were sold by the piece, or by number; the size or quality was often specified. The pay of artisans, teachers and lawyers was reckoned by the time or by the services; and the same was true of charges for transportation and the like.

2. It is regrettable that the price of wheat is lost on the record; when it is mentioned at other times in Roman history, it is chiefly in times of scarcity or of over-abundance. Thus in 210 B.C., during the second Punic War, wheat rose to $1.67 per bushel (Polybius, *History* IX, 45.3), while the poet Martial, in 101 A.D., speaks of a harvest so plentiful that wheat sold at 17 cents per bushel (Martial, *Epigrams*, XII, 76). But the real interest in these prices is not in their absolute value, but in their relation to wages paid at that time.

3. Many of these workers seem poorly paid in relation to the price of food, but we should note that most of them are furnished with their meals by the employer.

160

Appendix C

A Tax-Based Incomes Policy (TIP): What's It All About?

As the reader will have seen by now, wage and price controls have been employed by governments for centuries in many different countries and under many different forms. A particular variation of wage and price controls which many economists believe may be introduced in the United States (and elsewhere) in the near future has been called "Tax-Based Incomes Policy" or TIP for short. An especially cogent article explaining how this variation might work was written for the *Federal Reserve Bank of St. Louis Review* by a young economist at that Bank, Nancy Ammon Jianakoplos. The article appeared in their February 1978 issue and is republished here by permission.

Subject corporations to higher corporate income tax rates if they give pay raises which are too large. This is the essence of a plan devised by Governor Henry C. Wallich of the Federal Reserve Board and Sidney Weintraub of the University of Pennsylvania.[1] Their proposal to use the tax system to curb inflation is called "TIP," an acronym for tax-based incomes policy. As inflation continues to plague the economy, many economists feel that the traditional tools of monetary and fiscal policy are inadequate to handle the situation and have recommended direct measures to stop wage and price increases.[2] The Wallich-Weintraub plan has received considerable attention as a policy measure which might be capable of dealing with the problem of inflation.[3]

Before adopting a program such as TIP, it is important to understand clearly how the proposal would operate and, more importantly, whether it would achieve the desired results. The first part of this article describes the functioning of TIP and the rationale for such a program as envisioned by Wallich and Weintraub. The rest of the article is devoted to an assessment of whether TIP would accomplish its stated objectives.

[1] Wallich and Weintraub first collaborated on this idea in Henry C. Wallich and Sidney Weintraub, "A Tax-Based Incomes Policy," *Journal of Economic Issues* (June 1971), pp. 1-19.

[2] See, for example, "Another Weapon Against Inflation: Tax Policy," *Business Week*, October 3, 1977, pp. 94-96; "Debate: How to Stop Inflation," *Fortune* (April 1977), pp. 116-20; Lindley H. Clark, Jr., "Uneasy Seers: More Analysts Predict New Inflation Spiral or Recession in 1978," *Wall Street Journal*, December 2, 1977.

[3] See, for example, U.S. Congress, Congressional Budget Office, *Recovery With Inflation*, July 1977, p. 40; U.S. Congress, Joint Economic Committee, *The 1977 Midyear Review of the Economy*, 95th Cong., 1st sess., September 26, 1977, p. 76; "Well-Cut Taxes Should Be Tailored," *New York Times*, December 21, 1977.

How Would Tip Operate?

According to the plan presented by Wallich and Weintraub, TIP would be centered on a single wage guidepost established by the Government.[4] The acceptable percentage wage increase could be set somewhere between the average increase in productivity throughout the economy (asserted to be around 3 percent) and some larger figure which incorporates all or part of the current rate of inflation. The ultimate aim of the guidepost is to bring wage increases in line with nationwide productivity increases.

The TIP guidepost is directed at wages only, although the tax is levied on corporate profits. The basic assumption behind TIP is that monetary and fiscal policies have been ineffective because they have not been able to prevent labor from obtaining wage increases in excess of productivity gains, even when there is significant unemployment in the economy. Furthermore, Wallich and Weintraub contend that empirical evidence supports the view that price increases have been a constant markup over unit wage increases. Therefore, if wage increases can be kept down, price increases will also be held down.

The corporate income tax system would be employed to enforce the TIP guidepost. Corporations which grant wage increases in excess of the guidepost would be subject to higher corporate income tax rates based on the amount that wage increases exceed the guidepost.

In order to understand how TIP would operate, consider the following example. Suppose the guidepost for wage increases is set at, say, 5 percent for a particular year. In the base year, Corporation A had a total wage bill of $100,000 and in the following year granted increases which brought its total wage bill to $108,000—an 8 percent increase. Assuming no change in either the number or composition of the employees, this 8 percent increase is 3 percentage points above the guidepost. This excess would then be multiplied by a penalty number. If, for instance, the penalty was set at 2, the corporate tax rate of Corporation A would be increased by 6 percentage points (3 percentage point excess times penalty number of 2). Thus, instead of paying 48 percent of its profits in taxes, the existing corporate tax rate, Corporation A would have to pay 54 percent of its profits, as a penalty for acceding to "excessive" wage demands.

Wallich and Weintraub argue that because of competitive forces this

<hr>

[4]Unless otherwise noted, all descriptions of TIP in this article are based on Wallich and Weintraub, "A Tax-Based Incomes Policy"; Henry C. Wallich, "Alternative Strategies for Price and Wage Controls," *Journal of Economic Issues* (December 1972), pp. 89-104; Henry C. Wallich, "A Plan for Dealing With Inflation in the U.S.," *Washington Post*, August 21, 1977; Sidney Weintraub, "An Incomes Policy to Stop Inflation," *Lloyds Bank Review* (January 1971), pp. 1-12; and Sidney Weintraub, "Incomes Policy: Completing the Stabilization Triangle," *Journal of Economic Issues* (December 1972), pp. 105-22.

additional tax could not be shifted forward to prices.[5] They, therefore, believe that such a tax penalty would cause corporations to deal more firmly with labor. In their view the penalty would ultimately restrain the rate of wage increases and, hence, reduce the rate of inflation.[6] Since wage increases would be curbed, corporations would not have higher costs to pass through in the form of price increases, thereby eliminating a major "cost-push" element of inflation. Furthermore, since the increases in incomes of workers would more closely approximate increases in productivity, there would be smaller increases in spending, reducing the "demand-pull" aspect of inflation.

Wallich and Weintraub acknowledge certain difficulties in computing the corporation's wage bill. One method which they believe would overcome many of these difficulties would be to construct an index of wages, rather than using the gross dollar figure. Using this method, wages, fringe benefits, and other related payments would be computed for each job classification and skill level and divided by the hours worked at each level. These wage figures would then be combined into an index weighted by the proportion of each of these classifications in the entire corporation. Changes in this index would then be compared to the guidepost in order to assess whether the corporation would be penalized.

Administrative problems are not neglected by Wallich and Weintraub. They recognize that the tax laws must be specific and "airtight" in order to avoid loopholes. However, it is argued that TIP would not involve establishing a new bureaucracy. Most of the data necessary to administer TIP are already collected for corporate income tax and employee payroll tax purposes.

One of the principal merits of TIP, in the view of Wallich and Weintraub, is that it would not interfere with the functioning of the market system. They argue that there would be no direct controls or distortions to the pricing mechanism. Firms would still be free to grant large wage demands, but would face the penalty of a higher corporate tax rate.

Rather than a short-term plan to curb inflation, TIP is envisioned to be a long-term means of reducing the rate of price increase. However, TIP is not intended to function by itself. Both Wallich and Weintraub see it as

[5]See Richard A. Musgrave and Peggy B. Musgrave, *Public Finance In Theory and Practice* (New York: McGraw-Hill Book Company, 1973), Chapter 18, pp. 415-29, who contend that empirical evidence is inconclusive in determining whether the corporate income tax is shifted.

[6]Studies by Yehuda Kotowitz and Richard Portes, "The Tax on Wage Increases: A Theoretical Analysis," *Journal of Public Economics* (May 1974), pp. 113-32, and Peter Isard, "The Effectiveness of Using the Tax System to Curb Inflationary Collective Bargains: An Analysis of the Wallich-Weintraub Plan," *Journal of Political Economy* (May-June 1973), pp. 729-40, analyze the effect of TIP on an individual firm and conclude that theoretically TIP should lead to lower wage settlements for an individual firm.

a supplement to "appropriate" monetary and fiscal policies. In addition, if labor contends that TIP would hold down wages while allowing profits to increase, Wallich proposes the implementation of an excess profits tax. This could be accomplished by increasing the basic corporate tax rate to keep the share of profits in national income constant.[7]

Would Tip Work?

The TIP proposal has two principal objectives:
(1) to curb inflation, and
(2) to avoid interfering with the functioning of the market.

Given these aims of TIP, one can analyze whether TIP will, in fact, be able to accomplish its goals. Other issues raised by TIP, such as the costs of implementation and the ability of firms to avoid the tax penalty of TIP, will not be discussed here.[8]

Would TIP Curb Inflation?

TIP is based on the assumption that most of the inflation in the economy is of a "cost-push" nature. Inflation occurs, according to this framework, because labor is able to attain wage increases in excess of increases in productivity. Business is not capable of resisting, or finds it does not pay to resist, labor's demands. Faced with higher costs, businesses pass these costs through in the form of higher product prices. As prices rise, further wage increases are granted, forming the basis of a wage-price spiral. TIP is proposed as a measure which will intervene in this process and bring inflation to a halt.

As the Congressional Budget Office stated in a recent study, the assumption that inflation is the result of "cost-push" is "a conjectural notion at best."[8] A major challenge to the concept of "cost-push" rests on empirical evidence supporting an alternative theory of the cause of inflation. According to this other view, ongoing increases in the general price level (inflation) are primarily the result of excessive increases in the rate of

[7]Other adjuncts proposed for TIP include a payroll tax credit designed to entice workers to accept lower wages. See Lawrence S. Seidman, "A Payroll Tax-Credit to Restrain Inflation," *National Tax Journal* (December 1976), pp. 398-412.

[8]For a discussion of implementation problems, see Gardner Ackley, "Okun's New Tax-Based Incomes-Policy Proposal," Survey Research Center, Institute for Social Research, The University of Michigan, *Economic Outlook USA* (Winter 1978), pp. 8-9. Although Ackley deals with the anti-inflation proposal put forward by Arthur Okun, he notes that the critique also applies to the Wallich-Weintraub proposal.

[9]Congressional Budget Office, "Recovery With Inflation," p. 41.

monetary expansion.[10] Lags exist between the time when the money stock is increased and when prices rise. In this framework, the observed relationship between the rate of wage increase and the rate of price increase is explained as part of the adjustment process through which prices increase in response to increases in the money stock. This view does not deny the "cost-push" phenomenon, but contends that it is consistent with the view that inflation is ultimately caused by money growth.[11]

When the stock of money is increased faster than the rate of increase in production, people find themselves with larger cash balances than they desire to hold. In order to bring their cash balances down to desired levels, they will spend the money, thereby bidding up prices on goods and services, and the general price level will rise. As long as the stock of money increases faster than the demand for money, inflation will persist, even if TIP manages to hold down wages temporarily.

Conversely, just as inflation is caused by excessive growth of the money stock, the only way to stop inflation is to reduce the growth of the money stock. As the rate of monetary expansion is reduced, people will have cash balances below their desired levels. They will reduce their rate of spending in order to build up these balances. As spending (demand) falls, the rate of inflation will decrease. Prices are "sticky," and just as it took several years to build up the current rate of inflation, it will take several years for inflation to wind down. One of the by-products of reducing inflation is a temporary idling of resources, since prices do not tend to be flexible in the short run. This is a cost of reducing inflation which must be borne, just as there are costs imposed on society as inflation mounts.

The idea that there are certain "key" wages in society, such as union wages, to which other wages and prices adjust, confuses the *motivation* for increasing the money stock with the *cause* of inflation.[12] If certain unions are able to attain large wage increases, even in the face of falling demand, the prices of the products produced by this labor will increase. As prices increase, less of this product will be demanded and the use of the resources

[10]Empirical support of this view for the period 1955 to 1971 is presented by Leonall C. Andersen and Denis S. Karnosky, "The Appropriate Time Frame for Controlling Monetary Aggregates: The St. Louis Evidence," *Controlling Monetary Aggregates II: The Implementation*, Federal Reserve Bank of Boston, Conference Series No. 9, September 1972, pp. 147-77. Additional evidence for the period 1971 to 1976 is found in Denis S. Karnosky, "The Link Between Money and Prices—1971-76," this *Review* (June 1976), pp. 17-23.

[11]See Leonall C. Andersen and Denis S. Karnosky, "A Monetary Interpretation of Inflation" in Joel Popkin, ed., *Analysis of Inflation: 1965-1974*, Studies in Income and Wealth, Vol. 42, National Bureau of Economic Research, Inc. (Cambridge, Massachusetts: Ballinger Publishing Company, 1977), pp. 11-26.

[12]This argument draws on Armen A. Alchian and William R. Allen, *University Economics: Elements of Inquiry* (Belmont, California: Wadsworth Publishing Company, Inc., 1972), pp. 684-85.

(labor and capital) which produce this product will be decreased. Unemployment will rise as resources are freed to work in the production of other products whose prices are lower. The relative prices of products will change, but the average price level will be unchanged.

However, if the Federal Reserve policymakers keep a close watch on these "key" industries and see an increase in idle resources (unemployment) in these industries, they may take actions to alleviate the unemployment by increasing the money stock. The increases in spending resulting from monetary expansion will bid up average prices and return relative prices to a position similar to that prior to the granting of the wage demands. It was as a consequence of the excessive wage demands that policy actions were *motivated*, but it was monetary expansion which *caused* the subsequent inflation.

Some proponents of TIP base their support on the belief that TIP will reduce *expectations* of inflation. Lower expectations of inflation in the future, according to this view, will lead to lower demands for wage increases and eventually lower prices. However, expectations of inflation do not cause inflation.[13] It is ongoing inflationary forces in the economy, excessive rates of monetary expansion, which lead to expectations of future inflation. Curbing inflationary expectations requires curbing the underlying forces which cause them.

Wallich and Weintraub agree that TIP is a supplement to, not a substitute for, "appropriate" monetary and fiscal policy. However, the character of their "appropriate" monetary policy is questionable. In the basic article which outlined TIP, Wallich and Weintraub stated, ". . . the proposal is conceived as a supplement to the familiar monetary-fiscal policies so that the economy might operate closer to full employment without the inflationary danger of excess demand and 'overheating.'"[14] Indeed, in a later article Weintraub is more specific: "Given a suitable incomes policy to align wages (and salaries) to productivity, monetary policy would be released to make its contribution to full employment. . . . Full employment requires ample money supplies for its sustenance."[15] Thus, it appears that "appropriate" monetary policy, in the view of Wallich and Weintraub, is expansionary; however, a restrictive monetary policy is necessary to curb inflation.

This disparity in determining the appropriate character of monetary policy points out another problem with TIP. Given the lag time involved in the functioning of monetary policy, it might appear in the short run that TIP is, at least temporarily, holding down prices. If, at the same time,

[13]Weintraub supports this contention in Weintraub, "Incomes Policy: Completing the Stabilization Triangle," p. 116.

[14]Wallich and Weintraub, "A Tax-Based Incomes Policy," p. 1.

[15]Weintraub, "Incomes Policy: Completing the Stabilization Triangle," p. 110.

the Federal Reserve increases the rate of monetary expansion, inflationary pressures will actually be augmented. An incomes policy, such as TIP, gives policymakers the illusion of taking corrective measures against inflation when, in fact, reducing the rate of monetary expansion is the only way to accomplish that goal. In summary, it appears that TIP would not be effective in reducing inflation and could make matters worse by fostering inappropriate monetary policy.

Would TIP Interfere With the Market?

Wallich and Weintraub argue that TIP would not interfere with market pricing because no ceilings are placed on any wages or prices. TIP operates through the tax system, yet it is based on a *single* guidepost for every firm and industry. They contend that a single guidepost is appropriate because in competition all comparable workers would earn the same wage. TIP, therefore, is only imposing what competition would achieve.

The problem with this argument is that it is only true if all industries are in equilibrium and remain there. In a growing, changing economy, equilibrium prices and wage rates are changing. Prices and wages are constantly moving toward new equilibria: hence, there is no reason to believe that each sector in the economy would be at equilibrium when TIP was imposed or would remain there afterward. In the U.S. economy, demands and tastes of consumers are constantly shifting and the technology and products offered by business are also changing. As a consequence, the equilibrium prices of some goods are rising (houses, for example) while others are falling (electronic calculators). In addition, some firms are growing, making large profits, and seeking additional labor, while others are declining, earning very little profit, and contracting their labor forces.

Imposing a single wage guidepost would distort the price system. It does not matter whether the guidepost is imposed through the tax system or by direct fines and penalties. Those firms which are growing or are adapting to changing consumer tastes have an incentive to hire scarce resources (capital and labor) away from other firms, but they would be penalized either through a lower rate of return, if they grant "excess" wage demands, or by a barrier to growth if they adhere to the guidepost. Consequently, in some instances labor would not be compensated in accord with the demand for its services. In other cases, firms would not be able to attract all the labor they desired. Relative prices would, therefore, be distorted by the establishment of a single guidepost for all firms and industries.

The TIP proposal would lead to a misallocation of resources. Prices, when allowed to operate freely, offer signals of where demand is increasing and where demand is falling. Resources move to those industries or firms where they will receive the highest compensation. The TIP proposal would obscure these price signals and, hence, resources would not move to where they would be used most efficiently. The economy would suffer since production would be lower than it would be otherwise.

The distortions in the economy caused by TIP could have a very long lasting effect. Capital (plant and equipment) is allocated by the market to those firms which have the highest rate of return. The TIP proposal would reduce the rates of return of those firms which are growing, and capital would not be adequately allocated to them. Capital generally tends to have a relatively long life. Once it is misallocated, as a result of TIP, it would not be easy to reallocate it to a more efficient use. Thus, TIP could have serious long-term consequences, as a result of the distortions it would cause in the price system.

Conclusion

TIP is an incomes policy designed to reduce inflation without interfering with the market system. The essence of the proposal is to subject corporations to higher corporate income tax rates if they granted pay increases in excess of a single Government-mandated guidepost.

TIP would not be successful in reducing the rate of inflation because it is based on the premise that inflation is largely a "cost push" phenomenon—higher wages leading to higher prices, which lead to still higher wages. Inflation, however, is caused primarily by excessive growth of the money stock. The TIP proposal, therefore, deals only with the symptoms of inflation, rather than attacking inflation at its root.

TIP would distort the market pricing system because the imposition of a single wage guidepost would not allow relative prices to adjust fully to change. This would lead to inefficiencies and a lower level of production than would be otherwise attainable.

Inflation is a serious problem, and there are no magic solutions. There may be a temporary reduction in the apparent rate of inflation with TIP, but eventually leaks will develop in the system and prices will rise anyway. The only way to stop inflation is to reduce the rate of monetary expansion.

NANCY AMMON JIANAKOPLOS

Appendix D

An Analysis of President Carter's Wage-Insurance Plan

On October 24, 1978, President Carter announced the latest phase of his anti-inflation campaign. In doing so, he sketched the outline (without precise details) of a new proposal. This was his wage-insurance plan, which would have to be enacted into law by the Congress since it would alter current tax laws. Two Walker Fellows in Economics at The Heritage Foundation (Eugene McAllister and Andrew Chalk) have written a brief analysis of this plan which appears below.

On the evening of October 24, 1978, President Carter introduced Phase II of his battle against inflation. The program consists of voluntary wage and price guidelines, a pledge to reduce the 1980 budget deficit, a promise to investigate the inflationary impact of government regulations, and a proposal for "real wage insurance."

Real wage insurance, conceived by Arthur Okun of the Brookings Institution, is designed to offer workers accepting wage contracts below a target some protection should inflation exceed the anticipated rate. Under the Carter proposal workers settling for an increase of less than 7 percent would receive a tax rebate based on the difference between the actual inflation rate and 7 percent. For instance, with an inflation rate of 9 percent, workers might expect a 2 percent rebate.

Prior to its announcement, much of the anti-inflation program had been reported and discussed by the press. This had provided organized labor ample opportunity to express its displeasure. The inclusion of real wage insurance was a bid by the President to overcome the expected ennui and to make the program more palatable to labor.

Skepticism of real wage insurance is based on a variety of factors. The cost of the program and barriers to its administration have been criticized. The selling point of the program is that it offers an incentive to comply with the guidelines. This, however, is a questionable assertion. In addition, concerned observers have asked: what is the value of real wage insurance when past wage and price controls have failed?

A major objection to the program is its cost. Current estimates vary from 5 to 10 billion dollars. These totals appear even more substantial in light of the pledge to lower the 1980 deficit to 30 billion dollars. The final cost will depend on who is included and to what extent coverage is provided.

Nearly two months after the announcement the Carter Administration has failed to answer several criticial questions. Does the program cover all workers accepting a wage increase of less than 7 percent? If so, the real wage insurance might become a general tax reduction. If not, the program would aid the urban worker but ignore the rural or self employed worker.

Is there to be a limit to the amount of coverage provided? For instance, are rebates to be limited to 3 percent regardless of the rate of inflation? Are fringe benefits to be included, and if so to what extent?

Finally, what is the time frame for the real wage insurance? New wage contracts are often negotiated several years into the future. An insurance program which covers only the first year will afford little protection and little incentive to comply. The actual life of the insurance program is critical, yet extremely difficult to determine.

These unresolved questions are merely samples of the administrative difficulties raised by any real wage insurance program. The uncertainty is heightened upon realization that the program must receive congressional approval.

The purpose of the real wage insurance is to offer labor an incentive for wage demand restraint. The effectiveness of such a policy, however, is doubtful.

For example, under a 7 percent guideline a union correctly anticipates a 9 percent rate of inflation. The members will be better off accepting a 9 percent contract than settling for 7 percent initially and later a 2 percent rebate. The reason for this is that under a 9 percent contract the member receives the inflation adjustment in his weekly paycheck rather than through a rebate in the next year. A dollar in the present is worth more than one in the future. This is particularly true in an inflationary environment.

In addition, the previous wage increase often serves as the basis for current or future negotiations. A smaller percentage increase not only lowers the range of future percentage increases, but also makes the wage base for future considerations smaller. Thus, there would seem to be an incentive to ignore real wage insurance from the standpoint of both present return and future gains.

Real wage insurance does not directly reduce inflation. Rather it is designed as an enhancement to wage and price controls. The feasibility of real wage insurance should be judged not only on its own merits, but also on the effectiveness of the wage and price controls. These considerations make the impact of the real wage insurance program extremely dubious.

ANDREW CHALK AND EUGENE McALLISTER

Selected Bibliography

Ackley, Gardner, "Roles and Limits of Incomes Policy," *Oriental Economist*, Vol. 42, April 1974, pp. 18–24.

*American Enterprise Institute, *A New Look at Inflation: Economic Policy in the Early 1970s*, American Enterprise Institute, Washington, D.C., 1973. (Presents the diverse opinions of distinguished scholars on developments in the American economy since the institution of direct wage and price controls in August 1971.)

American Enterprise Institute, *Essays on Indexation and Inflation*, American Enterprise Institute, Washington, D.C., 1974.
(Authors such as William Fellner and Milton Friedman examine possible answers to the problem of inflation, rather than the traditional, but ineffective, wage-stop policies.)

*American Institute for Economic Research, *The Failure of Price Controls*, American Institute for Economic Research, Research Report, December 3, 1974.
(An examination of the most recent attempt at price controls which concludes that the controls failed to halt increases in prices.)

Anderson, John, "The Cost of Controls," *Ripon Forum*, April 1, 1974.

Anderson, R. M., "Prospects of Success for Government Price-fixing in the United States," *Economic World*, January 5, 1918 (NS Vol. 15).

Ashley, W. J., *An Introduction to English Economic History and Theory*, Longmans, London, 1923–5.

Askin, A. and Kraft, J., *Econometric Wage and Price Models: Assessing the Impact of the Economic Stabilization Program*, New York, 1975.

*Backman, Jules, *Rationing and Price Controls in Great Britain*, Brookings Institution, Washington, D.C., 1943.
(Excellent, crisp, short survey of the effectiveness and deficiencies in the wartime control policies.)

Backman, Jules, *The Price Control and Subsidy Program in Canada*, Brookings Institution, Washington, D.C., 1943.
(Review of a particularly extensive network of controls.)

*Backman, Jules, *Adventures in Price Fixing*, Farrar and Rinehart, Menasha, Wisconsin, 1936.
(This excellent little book relates some case histories from a variety of countries in which price controls have been tried.)

Ballantine, A. A., "Prices According to Law," *Atlantic Monthly*, November 1915.

Balogh, Thomas, *Germany: An Experiment in 'Planning' by the 'Free' Price Mechanism*, Blackwell, Oxford, 1950.

171

Barnes, H., "The Backside of Sweden's Labour Policy," *Financial Times Scandinavian Newsletter*, May 1976.

Bezanson, Anne, *Prices and Inflation During the American Revolution*, University of Pennsylvania Press, 1951.

Bhatia, R. J. and Bouter, A. C., "A System of Governmental Wage Control— Experience of the Netherlands, 1945–60," in *IMF Staff Papers*, Vol. VIII, (3), December 1961.

Blackaby, F. (ed.), *An Incomes Policy for Britain*, Heinemann, London, 1972.

*Blough, Roger M., "Minimizing the Effect of Controls," *Monthly Labor Review*, Vol. 97, March 1974, pp. 39–42.

(Excerpted from a paper presented to the 26th annual meeting of the Industrial Relations Research Association and the American Economic Association in New York, December 1973. The former chairman of the U.S. Steel Corporation argues against controls.)

Bodkin, Ronald G. and Lerner, Abba P., *Two Lectures on the Wage-Price Problem*, University of British Columbia, Department of Economics, Vancouver, British Columbia, 1974.

Boeckh, August, *The Public Economy of the Athenians*, Little, Brown & Co., Boston, 1857.

Bolles, Albert, *The Financial History of the United States*, Appleton & Co., New York, 1896.

Booth, Arch N., *Wage-Price Controls: The Challenge to Learn from History*, Chamber of Commerce of the U.S., Washington, D.C., 1975.

*Bourne, Henry, "Maximum Prices in France," *American Historical Review*, October 1917.

*Bourne, Henry, "Food Control and Price-fixing in Revolutionary France," *Journal of Political Economy*, February 1919.

Bowley, Arthur Lyon, *Prices and Wages in the United Kingdom, 1914–1920*, Oxford University Press, 1921.

(Well-documented and readable review of the wartime experience with controls.)

Bresciani-Turroni, C., *The Economics of Inflation*, 1931; English edition, Augustus Kelly, New York, 1968.

Brittan, Samuel, *Capitalism and the Permissive Society*, Macmillan, London, 1973.

Brittan, Samuel, *Second Thoughts on Full Employment Policy*, Centre for Policy Studies, London, 1975.

*Brittan, Samuel and Lilley, Peter, *The Delusion of Incomes Policy*, Temple Smith, London, 1977.

Brown, F., *Soviet Trade Unionism and Labor Relations*, Harvard University Press, 1966.

Brown, W. and Sisson, K., *A Positive Incomes Policy*, Fabian Society, London, 1976.

Buchanan, J., *The Limits of Liberty*, University of Chicago Press, 1975.

Burns, A. R., *Money and Monetary Policy in Early Times*, A. A. Knopf, New York, 1927.

Cagan, Phillip, *The Hydra-Headed Monster—The Problem of Inflation in the United States*, American Enterprise Institute, Washington, D.C., 1974.

Carlson, J. and Parkin, M., "Inflation Expectations," *Economica*, May 1975.

Carr, Willard Z., Jr.; Heinke, Rex S.; Ryan, Michael D., "A Short Historical Perspective of Economic Controls in the United States," *Business Lawyer*, Vol. 33, November 1977, pp. 3–28.

Chen, Huan-chang, *The Economic Principles of Confucius and his School*, Longmans, New York, 1911.

*Chin, Felix and Knight, Edward, *Government Policy Relating to Wages and Prices, 1974: A Selected Bibliography*, Library of Congress, Congressional Research Service, Washington, D.C., 1976.
(Excellent and extensive bibliography on both sides of the issue.)

Conference Board Economic Forum, *Inflation in the United States: Causes and Consequences*, New York, 1974.
("General View of Inflation," by A. Greenspan; "Inflation and Monetary Policy," by J. O'Leary; "Fiscal Policies and Inflation," by M. Weidenbaum; "Wage and Price Policies," by A. Rees; "Inflation and Free Enterprise," by C. J. Grayson, Jr.)

Conquest, R., *Industrial Workers in the USSR*, New York, Praeger, 1967.

*Darby, M., "The US Economic Stabilisation Programme 1971–74," in *The Illusion of Price and Wage Control*, Fraser Institute, Vancouver, 1976

Deutscher, Isaac, "Soviet Trade Unions," Hyperion Press, Westport, Connecticut, 1973.

Donnithorne, Audry, "China's Anti-inflationary Policy," *Three Banks Review*, No. 103, September 1974, pp. 3–25.

Dorfman, G., *Wage Politics in Britain*, Iowa State University Press, Ames, 1973.

The Economist, "Why Not Let It Alone?", *The Economist*, London, Vol. 89, September 6, 1919.

Edgren, G., *et al.*, "Wages, Growth and Distribution of Income," *Swedish Journal of Economics*, September 1969.

Edwards, Chilperic, *The Hammurabi Code and the Sinaitic Legislation*, Kennikat Press, Port Washington, N.Y., 1904.

Erhard, Ludwig, *Prosperity Through Competition*, Praeger, New York, 1958.

Elvander, N., "Collective Bargaining and Incomes Policy in the Nordic Countries: A Comparative Analysis," *British Journal of Industrial Relations*, November 1974.

Eucken, W., "On the Theory of the Centrally Administered Economy," *Economica*, May 1948.

Fakiolas, R., "Problems of Labor Mobility in the USSR," *Soviet Studies*, 14 July 1962.

Finley, M. I., *The Ancient Economy*, Chatto & Windus, London, 1973.

*Fisher, Antony, *Fisher's Concise History of Economic Bungling*, Caroline House, Ottawa, Ill., 1978.

(Published in England under the title *Must History Repeat Itself?*, London: Churchill Press, 1974).

Fisher, Irving, "A Statistical Relation Between Unemployment and Price Changes," *International Labour Review*, June 1926.

Franck, Louis, *French Price Control From Blum to Petain*, The Brookings Institution, Washington, D.C., 1942.

*Fraser Institute, *The Illusion of Wage and Price Control*, Vancouver, Canada, 1976.

*Friedman, Milton (ed.), *Studies in the Quantity Theory of Money*, University of Chicago Press, Chicago, 1956.

*Friedman, Milton, "What Price Guideposts?" in Shultz, George P. and Aliber, Robert Z., *Guidelines, Informal Controls and the Marketplace*, University of Chicago Press, Chicago, 1966.

*Friedman, Milton, *The Optimum Quantity of Money*, Aldine Press, Chicago, 1969.

*Friedman, Milton, *Unemployment Versus Inflation*, Institute of Economic Affairs, London, 1975.

*Friedman, Milton and Schwartz, A., *A Monetary History of the United States 1867–1960*, Princeton, 1963.

Fulton, Betty F., "Price Controls: An Elusive Panacea," *Wage-Price Law & Economics Review*, Vol. 2, No. 2, 1977, pp. 41–45 and 47–48.

Galbraith, J. K., *Money*, Andre Deutsch, London, 1975.

Garrett, Paul Willard, *Government Control Over Prices*, Government Printing Office, for the War Trade Board and the War Industries Board, Washington D.C., 1920.

(Comprehensive review of the American experiences with controls during World War I.)

Ghali, Moheb A., "The Effect of Controls on Wages, Prices, and Strike Activity," *Journal of Economics and Business*, Vol. 30, Fall 1977, pp. 23–30.

Gibbon, Edward, *The Decline and Fall of the Roman Empire*, W. Strahan & T. Cadell, London 1783–89.

Goodwin, C. (ed), *Exhortation and Controls*, Brookings Institution, Washington, 1975.

Gould, J. D., *The Great Debasement*, Clarendon Press, Oxford, 1970.

Gray, H. L., *War Time Control of Industry*, Macmillan, New York, 1918.

*Grayson, C. J., "The U.S. Economic Stabilisation Programme, 1971–74," in *The Illusion of Price and Wage Control*, Fraser Institute, Vancouver, 1976.

174

Grayson, C., "Controls Are Not the Answer," *Challenge*, Vol. 17, November–December 1974, pp. 9–12.

*Grayson, C., *Confessions of a Price Controller*, Dow-Jones, Irwin, New York, 1974.

Griffiths, Brian, *Inflation*, Weidenfeld, London, 1976.

Guillebaud, C., *The Economic Recovery of Germany, 1933–38*, Macmillan, London, 1939.

Hardy, Charles O., *Wartime Control of Prices*, Brookings Institution, Washington, D.C., 1940.

Harper, F. A., *Stand-by Controls*, Foundation for Economic Education, Irvington-on-Hudson, N.Y., 1953.

Harlow, Ralph, *Economic Conditions in Massachusetts During the American Revolution*, J. Wilson & Son, Cambridge, Mass., 1918.

*Hayek, F. A., *The Constitution of Liberty*, Routledge, London, 1960.

Hayek, F. A., *Choice in Currency*, Institute of Economic Affairs, London, 1975.

Hayek, F. A., *The Mirage of Social Justice*, Routledge, London, 1976.

*Hayek, F. A., *A Tiger by the Tail*, Institute of Economic Affairs, London, 1971. (Excellent series of essays and articles which testifies that "open" inflation [where one can see the rising prices] is better than "repressed" inflation [where the rises are disguised under a series of price and wage controls].)

Hensel, Struve and McClung, Richard, "Profit Limitation Controls Prior to the Present War," *Law and Contemporary Problems*, Duke University, Autumn 1943.

Hicks, Sir John, *A Theory of Economic History*, Clarendon Press, Oxford, 1969.

Hirsch, Julius, *Price Control in the War Economy*, Harper & Bros. Publishers, New York, 1943.

Howell, Ralph, M.P., "Low Pay and Taxation," *Low Pay Paper No. 8*, Low Pay Unit, London, 1976.

*Hunter, Laurence C., "British Incomes Policy, 1972–1974," *Industrial and Labor Relations Review*, Vol. 29, October 1975, pp. 67–84. (This Scottish economist demonstrates that the policy of the British government under the Heath administration did not achieve its wage and price goals and he notes that other government policies were working at cross-purposes by producing inflation.)

Hunter, Sir William Wilson, *Annals of Rural Bengal*, Smith, Elder, London, 1897.

Hutt, W. H., *The Strike Threat System*, Arlington House, New Rochelle, N.Y., 1973.

*Institute of Economic Affairs, *Verdict on Rent Control*, Institute of Economic Affairs, London, 1972.

(Highly recommended little book with contributions from many countries and many distinguished economists, such as F. W. Paish, Milton Friedman, George Stigler, and Bertrand de Jouvenal.)

Institute of Economic Affairs, *The Long Debate on Poverty*, Institute of Economic Affairs, London, 1973.

Jacobstein, Meyer and Moulton, Harold G., *Effects of the Defense Program on Prices, Wages and Profits*, Brookings Institution, Washington, D.C., 1941.

Jay, Peter, *Employment, Inflation and Politics*, Institute of Economic Affairs, London, 1975.

*Jefferson, Michael, *et al.*, *Inflation*, John Calder (Publishers) Ltd., London, 1977.

Jewkes, John, *The New Ordeal by Planning*, Macmillan, London, 1967.

Johnson, E. A. J., *American Economic Thought in the Seventeenth Century*, Russell & Russell, New York, 1961.

Johnston, T., *Collective Bargaining in Sweden*, Allen & Unwin, London, 1962.

Jones, A. H. M., *The Roman Economy*, Rowman and Littlefield, Totowa, N.J., 1974.

Jones, A., *The New Inflation*, Andre Deutsch, London, 1973.

Joseph, Sir Keith, Bt., *Reversing the Trend—a Critical Reappraisal of Conservative Economic and Social Policies*, Barry Rose, London, 1975.

*Kent, Roland, "The Edict of Diocletian Fixing Maximum Prices," *The University of Pennsylvania Law Review*, 1920.
(Objective review of Diocletian's economic troubles and the results of his wage and price control legislation; includes the complete preamble to the Edict plus a sample of actual rates.)

Keynes, J. M., *A Treatise on Money*, Vol. 2, 1930, new edition, Macmillan, London, 1975.

Kirsch, L., *Soviet Wages*, MIT Press, Cambridge, Mass., 1972.

Kirzner, I., *Competition and Entrepreneurship*, University of Chicago Press, Chicago, 1973.

Kosters, M., *Controls and Inflation—The Economic Stabilization Programme in Retrospect*, American Enterprise Institute, Washington, D.C., 1975.

*Lacy, Mary G., *Food Control During Forty-six Centuries*, Address before the Agricultural Society, Washington, D.C., March 16, 1922. First published in *Scientific Monthly*, June 1923, reprinted by Foundation for Economic Education, Irvington-on-Hudson, N.Y.

Laidler, David, "The 1974 Report of the President's Council of Economic Advisors. The Control of Inflation and the Future of the International Monetary System," *American Economic Review*, Vol. 64, September 1974.
(Argues that wage and price controls failed because monetary policy was inconsistent with their success in the U.S. economy. In the international sphere, the author argues that the real issues involved in reforming the international monetary system concern the extent to which individual countries can be expected to coordinate their domestic stabilization plans.)

Lanzillotti, R., *Phase II in Review: The Price Commission Experience*, Brookings Institute, Washington, D.C., 1975.

Leites, Kussiel, *Recent Economic Developments in Russia*, Oxford University Press, New York, 1922.

*Lekachman, Robert, "The Case for Controls," *The New Republic*, October 14, 1978, p. 18.

Levy, Jean-Philippe, *The Economic Life of the Ancient World*, University of Chicago, 1967.

(Insightful short economic history of Egypt, Greece and Rome, with analyses of various government regulations.)

*Lewis, David and Sharpe, Myron E., "The Great Debate on Wage-Price Controls," *Challenge*, Vol. 17, January–February 1975, pp. 26–32.

Lipsey, R. and Parkin, M., "Incomes Policy: A Reappraisal," *Economica*, May 1970.

Litman, Simon, *Prices and Price Control in Great Britain and the United States During the World War*, Oxford University Press, 1920.

Meiselman, David I., "In Defense of Floating Rates: U.S. Inflation Must Be Labelled 'Made In The U.S.' Rather Than 'Imported'," *The Wall Street Journal*, September 13, 1974.

*Meiselman, David I., "Worldwide Inflation: A Monetarist View," in *The Phenomenon of Worldwide Inflation*, AEI, Washington, D.C., 1975.

Menderhausen, H., "Prices, Money and Distribution of Goods in Post-War Germany," *American Economic Review*, June 1949.

Merlin, S., "Trends in German Economic Controls Since 1933," *Quarterly Journal of Economics*, February 1943.

Merritt, A. N., *War Time Control of Distribution of Food*, Macmillan, New York, 1920.

Mills, Daniel Q., *Government, Labor and Inflation, Wage Stabilization in the United States*, Chicago University Press, Chicago, 1975.

*Mills, Daniel Q., "Some Lessons of Price Controls in 1971–73," *Bell Journal of Economics*, Vol. 6, Spring 1975, pp. 3–49.

(Very good review of the ineffectiveness of the Nixon controls and some useful theoretical comments on the nature and effect of price controls.)

Minchinton, W. E. (ed.), *Wage Regulation in Pre-Industrial England*, David & Charles, London, 1972.

Mitchell, Daniel J. B., "Wage and Price Controls: Past and Future," *Pittsburgh Business Review*, Vol. 46, Winter 1976, pp. 5–11.

Moulton, Harold G. and Schlotterbeck, Karl T., *Should Price Control Be Retained?*, Brookings Institution, Washington, D.C., 1945.

(Pamphlet which examines the need and value of continuing controls after the war effort.)

Nathan, Otto, *The Nazi Economic System*, Duke University Press, Durham, N.C., 1944.

177

Olds, Irving S., *The Price of Price Controls*, Foundation for Economic Education, Irvington-on-Hudson, N.Y., 1952.

Otani, Ichiro, "Some Empirical Evidence on the Determinants of Wage and Price Movements in Japan, 1950–1973: a Survey," *International Monetary Fund Staff Papers*, Vol. 22, July 1975.

Outhwaite, R. B., *Inflation in Tudor and Early Stuart England*, Macmillan, London, 1969.

Paulus, J. D., "Experience with Wage and Price Controls in the United States," Board of Governors of the Federal Reserve System, Paper presented at the eleventh meeting of Economists of Central Banks of the American Continent, Quito, Ecuador, November 1974.

*Pepper, G. and Wood, G. F., *Too Much Money*, Institute of Economic Affairs, London, 1976.

Phelps, E. S., "Phillips Curves, Expectations of Inflation and Optimal Unemployment of Time," *Economica*, August 1967.

Phelps-Brown, E. H., "Guidelines for Growth and for Incomes in the United Kingdom," in Shultz, G. P. and Aliber, R. Z. (eds.), *Guidelines, Informal Controls, and the Market Place*, University of Chicago Press, 1966.

Philip, A. J., *Rations, Rationing and Food Control*, Book World, London, 1918.

Phillips, A. W., "The Relationship Between Unemployment and the Rate of Change of Money Wages in the UK, 1861–1957," *Economica*, 1958, pp. 783–91. Reprinted in *Inflation*, Ball and Doyle (eds.), Penguin, London, 1969.

Postan, M. H., *The Medieval Economy and Society*, Weidenfeld, London, 1972.

Pounds, N. G. J., *An Economic History of Medieval Europe*, Longman, London, 1974.

Rasin, Alois, *Financial Policy of Czechoslovakia During the 1st Year of its History*, Carnegie Endowment for International Peace, New York, 1923.

Reinfeld, Fred, *The History of Civil War Money*, Sterling, New York, 1959.

*Reynolds, Alan, "The Case Against Wage and Price Control," *National Review*, September 24, 1971.

Royal Commission on the Distribution of Income and Wealth (Diamond Commission) HMSO London: Report No. 1, *Initial Report*, 1975; Report No. 2, *Income from Companies*, 1975; Report No. 3, *Higher Incomes from Employment*, 1976.

Rostovtseff, M., *The Social and Economic History of the Roman Empire*, Oxford University Press, 1957.

Schiff, Eric, *Incomes Policies Abroad*, American Enterprise Institute, Washington, D.C., 1971/1972.
(Two volumes giving a clear and readable review of the incomes policies operating in the United Kingdom, the Netherlands, Sweden, France, West

Germany, Austria, Denmark, and Canada. Informative and useful; the broad conclusion is that controls have not been made to work in any of those countries, although some have attained a measure of success with other policies.)

*Shenoy, Sudha (ed.), *Wage-Price Control: Myth and Reality*, The Centre for Independent Studies, Turramurra, Australia, 1978.

Shultz, George P. and Dam, Kenneth W., "Reflections on Wage and Price Controls," *Industrial and Labor Relations Review*, Vol. 30, January 1977, pp. 139–151.

Shultz, George P. and Aliber, Robert Z., *Guidelines, Informal Controls and the Marketplace*, University of Chicago Press, Chicago, 1966.

Simes, Dimitri K., "The Soviet Parallel Market," in *Survey*, Vol. 21, No. 3, 1975.

*Skousen, Mark, *Playing the Price Controls Game*, Arlington House, New Rochelle, New York, 1977.

Smith, Lawrence B., "Canada's Incomes Policy: An Economic Assessment," *Canadian Tax Journal*, Vol. 24, January–February 1976, pp. 67–73.

*Stein, Herbert, "Waiting for Phase II," *The AEI Economist*, October 1978.

Stein, Herbert with Benjamin Stein, *On the Brink*, Simon and Schuster, New York, 1977.

Sutch, W. B., *Price Fixing in New Zealand*, Columbia University Press, New York, 1932.

(Excellent book about the effects of New Zealand's experiments with price controls during and after the First War. Many sectors of the economy are examined, but the single lesson is clear: the side-effects of controls are worse than the problem they are intended to cure.)

*Turin, S. P., "Market Prices and Controlled Prices of Food in Moscow," *The Royal Statistical Society Journal*, London, May 1920.

Taylor, K. W., "Canadian Wartime Price Controls—1941–46," *Canadian Journal of Economics and Political Science*, February 1947.

Ulman, Lloyd and Flanagan, Robert J., *Wage Restraint: A Study of Incomes Policies in Western Europe*, University of California Press, Berkeley, 1971.

U.S. Congressional Budget Office, *Income Policies in the United States: Historical Review and Some Issues*, Washington, D.C., 1977, 80 pages (U.S. Congressional Budget Office, Background paper).

*Walker, Michael (ed.), *Which Way Ahead: Canada After Wage and Price Control*, The Fraser Institute, Vancouver, Canada, 1977.

Walters, A. A., *Money in Boom and Slump*, 3rd edition, Institute of Economic Affairs, London, 1971.

Webster, Pelatiah, *Political Essays*, J. Crukshank, Philadelphia, 1791.

(Webster is generally regarded as the first American economist of note; his works include a good many comments on the price and wage controls of his time.)

White, Andrew Dickson, *Fiat Money Inflation in France*, 1912, modern edition, Foundation for Economic Education, Irvington-on-Hudson, New York, 1959.

Whiteman, Charles H., "A New Investigation of the Impact of Wage and Price Controls," *Federal Reserve Bank of Minneapolis Quarterly Review*, Vol. 2, Spring 1978, pp. 2–8.

Wilkinson, H. L., *State Regulation of Prices in Australia*, Melville & Mullen, Melbourne, 1917.
(Good review of the early Australian experiences with controls, related in this "treatise on price fixing and state socialism.")

Windmuller, J. P., *Labor Relations in the Netherlands*, Cornell University Press, 1969.

Wootton, B., *Social Foundations of Wages Policy*, Allen & Unwin, 1962.

Worswick, G. D. N. (ed.), *The Concept and Measurement of Involuntary Unemployment*, Allen & Unwin, 1976.

Yeager, Leland B., *International Monetary Relations*, Harper & Row, New York, 1966.

*Asterisk indicates an especially useful work.

Index

A Final Comment
on the Good Intentions
of Government

"The President has stressed repeatedly the
value of simplicity of government documents
and the importance of not placing undue
reporting burdens on the public."
Fact Book: Wage and Price Standards, p. 20.
(Published by the Council on Wage and Price
Stability on October 31, 1978).

(continued on last page)

The Results
of the Good Intentions
# of Government

$$P_{75} = \left[3.00 \times \left(\frac{60}{450} \right) \right] + \left[2.00 \times \left(\frac{50}{450} \right) \right] + \left[34.00 \times \left(\frac{340}{450} \right) \right] = \$26.31$$

$$P_{77} = \left[4.00 \times \left(\frac{60}{450} \right) \right] + \left[1.60 \times \left(\frac{50}{450} \right) \right] + \left[39.75 \times \left(\frac{340}{450} \right) \right] = \$30.74$$

Fact Book: Wage and Price Standards, 1978, page 30, how to calculate company-wide average price.

$$\left[\left(\frac{W_T}{W_o} \right) \frac{1}{T} - 1 \right] \times 100 \leq 7.0$$

Ibid., page 24, how to compute pay standard for collective bargaining agreements.

$$P(t) = \sum_i \left[P_i(t) \times \left(\frac{R_i}{\Sigma_j R_j} \right) \right]$$

Ibid., page 27, how to figure company-wide average price in any quarter.